Essential BUSINESS Websites

Don't Miss the eBook

WebPointers Essential Business Websites
is also published as an "eBook" and your purchase
of this printed edition entitles you to download
the free Electronic Edition in Adobe Software's PDF Format.
The Electronic Edition is identical in appearance to the
Printed Edition you now hold in your hands but all
Internet hyperlinks are active — a simple click
will take you to the Website mentioned.
In addition, the Table of Contents, Subject Index and
complete Appendix of Websites are also hyperlinked.
For download instructions please register your copy of
WebPointers Essential Business Websites at:

http://www.webpointers.com/register.html

Welcome to the exciting world of Internet Exploration.
Feedback is welcome.

Email: catbird@webpointers.com

WebPointers

Essential BUSINESS Websites

Kitty Williams & Robin Lind
catbird@webpointers.com

Hope Springs Press
2000

An original WebPointers™ Interactive Internet Guide
Published by Hope Springs Press

Portions of this book originally appeared in newspapers acting in syndication
with Hope Springs Press and on WebPointers Online
http://www.webpointers.com

Printed in the United States of America
© 2000 Hope Springs Press Inc
All rights reserved.

ISBN 0-9639531-3-3

Library of Congress Catalogue Card Number - 98-70568

1 2 3 4 5 6 7 8 9 0

Contents

Entrepreneurs

Financial Planning

Management

Mind Candy

Reference

Technology

Preface

If you're new to the World Wide Web, welcome! This extraordinary medium is revolutionizing the way we all do business and if your business isn't yet online it soon will be.

The world's economy is changing; it is being transformed by information-based industries. The velocity of change is accelerating. How you work and how you live will be determined by how you respond to the increasing pace of change.

You are also an agent for change. The way you respond to what you find (and what you need) will help determine the next stages of evolutionary — and revolutionary — business development.

This book savors the essence of business on the Web. Exploring the sites gathered here will give you a quick understanding of basic techniques you can use to put the Web to work for you.

WebPointers Essential Business Websites is a book in the vanguard of change: it includes a free electronic edition — an "eBook." Please take a moment to register for your password at Web-Pointers Online and download the eBook in Adobe Software's PDF format. It includes active hyperlinks to every Website mentioned as well as the Table of Contents, Appendix and Index.

The printed book is a powerful tool that has demonstrated its usefulness for more than 550 years. The eBook is an infant that offers dynamic internal referencing and external connectivity to the Internet. The combination of print and pixel is more powerful still.

We look forward to seeing you on the Web.

Cheers!

Kitty Williams and Robin Lind

catbird@webpointers.com

for

our parents

Alex, Anne, Joan and Murat

and for

our children

Frankie and Maria

Email Passes Telephone as Major Business Tool

"Worldwide email volume this year is expected to be four trillion (4 million x million) or about 10 billion per day."

Email, declared early on to be the Internet's "killer-app," is undoubtedly the greatest innovation in business in the past decade.

If you're in business and you're not using it yet, let this be a heads-up: going without email is not the same as not having a telephone. It's more akin to not having an address.

Am I kidding? Not in the slightest.

According to an American Management Association survey "... electronic mail has now overtaken the telephone as the primary means of business communication." Do I believe that? Of course. I got it by email.

Better than that, the email was written by Vin Crosbie, one of brightest and most thoughtful leaders in the Internet's rapidly-moving field of information delivery technologies.

He was writing to the general discussion list devoted to "Online News" — the Web-based versions of newspapers and magazines — hosted by Planetary News. There are about 1500 subscribers to the list from around the globe and, although most of them have never met face to face, many of them have been sharing news and debating ideas by email for several years.

Rarely has the exchange of ideas been so fruitful. Crosbie, whose company is located in Greenwich, CT, was responding to a query on an email discussion group from free-lance writer Stu Lowndes in Montreal, Quebec.

Lowndes sought some "quick and dirty" statistics on email usage and asked if he remembered correctly that it was "a figure like 15 million messages posted daily."

"You're only off by a few magnitudes," emailed Crosbie. "Worldwide email volume this year is expected to be four trillion (4 million x million) or about 10 billion per day."

That brought a response from another of the very brightest bulbs on the list, Curt Monash, editor of the Monash Software Letter (who earned his Ph.D. in Mathematics from Harvard at age 19). Monash thought Crosbie's figures were high and wanted some explanations.

Readers of the list were then treated to an on-going multi-logue over two days, that brought in a half-dozen knowledgeable contributors, and learned:

- in 1998 there were approximately 112 million home users of the Internet world-wide generating an estimated one billion emails a day
- there are approximately 110 million corporate users sending an estimated 20 emails each per day and receiving perhaps 40
- this amounted to an estimated 3.9 trillion emails in 1998
- by comparison, the US Post Office delivered 0.18 trillion envelopes and packages during 1996
- these figures don't include educational, government and military email use
- 62% of Canadians have access to computers, 36% to the Internet
- Finland has a higher per capita Internet penetration than the United States

We also had the treat of "meeting" new list-member Bonnie Scott, a recent Cornell graduate, who shows every promise of joining the ranks of the 1000-watt commentators.

"I've met more and more people who neither own their own computers nor have any regular access to them," emailed Scott, "yet they have Hotmail or Juno accounts and a GeoCities WebPage. These barely computer-literate friends are accomplishing the same things as folks with years of Internet experience and thousands of dollars for computer equipment..."

This discussion even prompted Online News list-owner Steve Outing to pipe in with the news that his logs showed the list had delivered 382,000 email messages during March, 1998.

If you're still a doubting Thomas on the email question you might want to subscribe to the free Internet Marketing newsletter published by Iconocast.

As early as 1996 their research indicated email was the most popular online activity for people accessing the Internet. They estimated 50% of the US population (135 million) will communicate by email by 2001 and the number of people worldwide using email will grow to 450 million, up from 60 million in 1997.

To view the whole discussion go to the Online News Page archives and search for the keywords "email statistics." You'll find the email conversation "threaded" into a yarn that tells the story of this amazing new medium.

Iconocast Internet Marketing Newsletter (http://www.iconocast.com/)
Online News Page archives (http://www.journalist.org/cgi-bin/online-news/)

"These barely computer-literate friends are accomplishing the same things as folks with years of Internet experience and thousands of dollars of computer equipment..."

Access Your Own Email from Anyone's Computer

Email has become such a part of modern business that its use can become an addiction.

Users who haven't been online for several hours exhibit withdrawal symptoms. The nervous drumming of finger tips, the perspiration on the upper lip, the eyes scanning any printed matter with repeated upward glances looking for the reply button ... you've seen them.

But it's not just the addicts who get desperate. If there's one thing that most business travelers would like to have in the new year it's a way to access their email anywhere in the world.

The cheap solution is to have an AOL account and dial in to AOL's local number when you get to the hotel and wait for that perky alert: "You have mail!"

The only downside is that you can't get your regular emails from your business Internet Service Provider (unless that is also AOL).

A more expensive alternative is a long distance call to your regular Internet Service Provider.

The cheapest solution is to have friends who let you use their computer and Internet connection, go online, open their browser, reconfigure their identity, password and Standard Mail Transfer Protocol log-on procedures to access your email as if you're on your own machine.

(Just remember to change all the settings — and restore them when you're finished. When I tried this recently on a trip to Chicago my wife was rather surprised to receive emails from "Jeremy" after I forgot to change the sender's name in the Settings menu.)

Travelers shouldn't need an engineering degree to get their email

The reason the cheapest solution works is because all email uses the same protocols. Once you're connected to the Internet, retrieving your email requires only your name and password, much the same as visiting your local post office; knowing the box number and combination to open the wee door gives you access to letters sent from anywhere in the world.

Travelers shouldn't need an engineering degree to get their email. You would think that someone would have focused on this universal set of protocols and made it easier already.

This being the Internet, where anything you can imagine has probably already been created by someone a few thoughts ahead of you, the possibility has actually been a reality for over a year now.

MailStart, a small Sacramento, CA company, now a subsidiary of BrandMakers Inc., has a simple Web-based solution that lets you check your own email anytime you go online from any* machine anywhere. No long distance charges. No monkeying around with settings. MailStart is not only simple, it's free.

Wherever you can access the Web, simply go to MailStart.com, enter your email address and password and click on "Check My Mail." Within moments you have access to all your messages and can read, reply, forward, organize messages in folders and even save drafts of outgoing emails until you're ready.

Because MailStart doesn't delete your email it's still on your own email provider when you get back home and, if you check the "cc me" box, you can also keep a record of your outgoing emails while you're on the road.

MailStart is a member of the TRUSTe privacy program and does not keep a record of your email address or password; the information is encrypted when sent over the Internet to re-trieve your emails and discarded when you log off.

MailStart launched MailStart Plus in early 1999 which offers the sort of robust email services that are currently found in fancy email programs such as Eudora, including a spell checker, address book, interactive online help and filters that allow you to sort incoming emails into folders based on from, to, date and subject — very handy if you'd like to automatically filter spam straight into trash!

MailStart (http://www.mailstart.com)

[* Although "all" email uses the same protocols, some companies keep their email behind "firewalls" and some services like AOL, MSN and AT&T have their own proprietary systems which don't comply with the universal standards; sorry guys, you're out of luck.]

... anything you can imagine has probably already been created by someone a few thoughts ahead of you

New Software Lets You Sign Your Emails

Trillions of email messages are now flying about on the Internet and it's about time for them to get a little bit more civilized.

You're never going to be able to send your emails on 100% cotton rag paper with an expensive watermark but how about signing your name in your own handwriting?

It's technically possible, of course: you could find a scanner and scan your signature into your computer as an image, then attach to your email file but that's pretty techie for both sender and recipient.

You could use a graphics program such as Microsoft Paint or Corel Draw to create a bitmap version of your signature but that's easier said than done for most of us.

Everytime I've tried to write my name using my mouse while watching the computer monitor, it looks worse. Not that I have great handwriting to start with, but it's my own and I'm used to it.

Even if you are very dextrous and can write beautifully with a mouse or some other attachment such as an electronic stylus, the resulting bitmapped files are huge. My simple five letter first name (looking like it had been written by a trained chimpanzee) took up 16.8MB of disk space! That's more space than my first computer had on its entire hard drive. Fugettaboudit.

Enter Signature-mail, an inexpensive ($14.95) software program that allows you to put your signature on emails or faxes. It's fun and easy to use and the signatures it provides take very little room so your correspondents won't get annoyed and give up before they let your email download.

The Signature-mail home page provides a form that can be printed out. I signed five versions of my name, from "Love, Mom" to my full legal name, in the spaces provided and faxed the page to an 800 number. (If you have even more personalities than I do, you can have up to 25 versions of your signature.)

... how about signing your name in your own handwriting?

The Frequently Asked Questions page suggested that I would get an email back with further instructions within a few minutes. It took about 90, which only seemed long because they got my hopes up. I checked my email every five minutes until it came…

The software took only five minutes to download — it's 1.2 megabytes — over my fast connection and it was up and running minutes later. If you read the directions, you'll find it very easy to use. It worked fine in Internet Explorer's Outlook Express, where it was integrated into the toolbar.

I had to change my Netscape mail so that it would send HTML mail before it worked very well with that, plus everytime I launch it to add a signature to a Netscape generated email, it throws up a grave warning of a high risk of mischief to my hard drive. I gulped and forged ahead.

It isn't integrated into AOL, but you can cut and paste your signature into an AOL 4.0 email.

Finally, if you're faxing from your word processor, you can cut & paste your signature right into the fax.

Did I mention that you can also change the color and size of the signature — you can. Fuchsia for a love note, perhaps, navy for the pen and ink effect.

Signature-mail is an Internet based company led by Michael Lloyd and Lee Browne. According to Tech Support and Help Desk maven Jim Sheldon-Dean they are "spread all over the country.

"I do tech support and develop and maintain the Help Desk from Vermont, and our Mac programmer also lives in the same small town. Michael and Lee are in two locations in Connecticut (at either end of the state), our lead Windows programmer is also from Connecticut, although he's now living near our network operations center, which is in Virginia. Our formal Quality Assurance team is in the SF Bay area, as is another of our managers. Our customers? They're all over the world!"

The software depends on some of the advances in general email technology and works with most of the major Windows-based programs.

The official Version 1.0 of Signature-mail for Windows was launched in early February of 1999; the Macintosh version was introduced in late summer.

Signature-mail (http://www.signature-mail.com/)

… you can also change the color and size of the signature … Fuchsia for a love note, perhaps, navy for the pen and ink effect.

love, Kitty

E-Cards Change Greeting Rules

Snail mail has been around since people shifted from carving marks on boulders to scratching notes on broken potsherds, which are infinitely more portable.

In conventional letter writing, whether the missives are delivered by hand, courier or government agent, there are traditions. Rules have evolved to govern both the medium and the message.

Take greeting cards. They can help if you need to say something and can't think how.

Some people would even have you believe that to send the very best you must use an illustrated, pre-printed and pre-written card with logo and copyright on the back. Racks and racks of them in every drug and grocery store demonstrate their widespread acceptance.

Email and the Internet have raised new questions — and new opportunities.

Is it permissible to invite people to dinner by email? Thank for a present? Send good wishes? Sometimes. It depends.

Should an email be treated as a letter or a phone call? Hard to say.

And if it's all right to commit sentiments of generosity or gratitude or good will to an electronic medium, how can you make it seem a little fancier? More elegant?

Even if your email software lets you change the colors and typefaces in your message, sometimes an email isn't enough.

Or at least, that's what the electronic greeting cards people hope. If you like old-fashioned cards, you don't have to give them up when you go online.

Admittedly there may be something a little odd about sending a picture (someone else drew) to illustrate a little doggerel (that someone else wrote) to a friend electronically but there are myriad sites offering e-greetings, some for a fee, others for free.

Some are quite entertaining, others are too much trouble to bother with.

If the e-greetings site is well designed and the "cards" load quickly, they will bring a smile. With a little animation and music added, they're even cuter. Your friends don't have to feel bad about throwing them out or recycling them.

Happy Chinese Moon Festival!

If you have completely forgotten a birthday or anniversary, a last minute electronic greeting might save your bacon. Or it might not...

One of the most successful is Blue Mountain Arts' free electronic greetings site with 40 categories of greetings, some for celebrations I suspect were invented on the spot by the Blue Mountain people.

Cards featured recently celebrated Chinese Moon Festival, Clergy Appreciation Day, Sukkot, Columbus/Native American Day, Bosses Day, Sweetest Day (!?), Diwali, and Hallowe'en.

There were also horse cards, cards to an ex-love, and "miss you" cards, cards with wolves, animated Shakespeare (the lines were moving up an down and made me seasick), and cards for a variety of other purposes.

Diwali, in case you didn't already know, is the Hindu festival of lights celebrated at the end of October, and also known as Deepavali. If you want more free e-cards for Diwali, you can find them at Tamil Pages' Deepavali Cards on the Internet.

A huge list of greeting card links is available from Olleyowl's Greetings Cards and Links site, compiled by an Australian mother of three and computer fanatic. She has a bunch of clever cards of her own you can send, as well.

But, through her list, I found a link to the e-card site for Hallmark, the freeworld leader of commercial greetings. After all the fun I had had with free cards, I was disappointed by that one.

Hallmark's cards were nice enough, as you would expect. There is a large selection of free cards as well as animated, musical cards you can pay $2.50 for. In order to send any of them, however, you need to sign up and give them a bit of information about yourself, which doesn't bother me too much. What did bother me was learning that all of my recipients reported problems with slow download time and difficulty finding my message.

When you care to send the very best I'd recommend you study the "free" market first.

Blue Mountain Arts (http://www.bluemountain.com/index.html)
Diwali (http://india.indiagov.org/culture/festival/diwali.htm)
Deepavali Cards (http://www.tamilpages.com/greetingcards/diwali.shtml)
Olleyowl (http://www.angelfire.com/ak/olly/greeting.html)
Hallmark (http://www.hallmarkconnections.com/)

... a last minute electronic greeting might save your bacon. Or it might not...

Your Own PC Can Create Postage Online

The appeal of customization is a major feature of the new programs

Many consumers and small business operators have used their computers and laserprinters for more than a decade to produce snappy-looking envelopes. Most have long realized that the same technology could be harnessed to put stamps on the envelopes without having to use a separate and expensive postage meter and a second mechanical process.

It was just a matter of waiting for the technology to be approved by the Postal Service.

In early August of 1999 the waiting ended as the USPS formally licensed two Internet companies, E-Stamp.com and Stamps.com, who immediately began selling what's called "PC Postage" over the Internet.

If you've got the basic home office equipment of PC, Laser or Inkjet printer and Internet connection, you can sign up, download software, buy postage and begin printing either envelopes or labels that have verified addresses, automatically-assigned nine-digit ZIP Codes and machine-readable bar codes that will speed your mail piece through automated equipment that doesn't require human handling.

The two Internet companies that won initial approval to provide postage to consumers online are E-Stamp.com and Stamps.com, both of California. Two bigger companies, Neopost and Pitney Bowes, continued in a beta testing program and were expected to be given full approval for their services a short time after according to Dr. Harry Whitehouse, president of Envelope Manager, and the engineer who originally presented the PC Postage concept to the USPS in late 1991.

Whitehouse's company teamed with NeoPost for the online postage business but also offers sophisticated mailing software programs including "Dazzle Designer" which allows illustrations and graphics to customize your mailings.

The appeal of customization is a major feature of the new programs, says Whitehouse, who has had his own rewarding experience sending out birthday invitations with his daughters' photos on the envelope; he doesn't preclude the possibility of the Post Office eventually permitting consumers to create their own "commemorative graphics" with a photo of family members or favorite pets.

"These are things that really make your mail stand out," he said. "Your mail can be as good as your design skills."

(At the time of original approval however, customization was delayed for further study; a feature on Stamps.com that allowed a company to place its own logo in the stamp location was curtailed after inappropriate graphics were reportedly used by an early tester.)

The real benefit to the consumer in all of these programs is the accompanying software that supports importing addresses from most major software programs, provides address verification, adds ZIP+4 coding and automatic machine-readable bar codes; the USPS benefits whenever mail can be processed automatically and moved speedily without human intervention.

E-Stamp offers a Starter Kit for $49.99 that includes $25 postage, a set of Avery labels, software on CD-ROM and a small electronic device (they call it an "electronic vault") about the size of a box of wooden matches that plugs into the back of your computer. Additional postage can be ordered online for cost plus a 10% "convenience" fee.

They also plan to offer a digital scale to weigh your mail which then calculates the amount of postage due according to weight and destination.

Stamps.com's version is free and doesn't require any special hardware. You download their software from the Internet, buy postage and you're ready to go. They offer the same address verification, ZIP+4 and bar coding as E-Stamp. Their "convenience" fees range from 10% to 15% based on amount of postage used.

It may seem odd to use computer technology that can send your electronic message instantly for free to print out postage on an old-fashioned paper envelope which has to be put into the mail and won't be delivered for several days but there is something special about a real letter. And how else can you get that check that's supposed to be "in the mail"?

E-stamp.com (http://www.e-stamp.com)
Stamps.com (http://www.stamps.com)
Neopost (http://www.neopost.com)
Pitney Bowes (http://www.pb.com)
Envelope Manager (http://www.envmgr.com)

... there is something special about a real letter. And how else can you get that check that's supposed to be "in the mail"?

Newest Websites Show Exciting Future Technologies

From time to time I run across people who still believe the Internet is a fad, the Web is a waste of time, and e-commerce is an over-hyped fraud pitched by scam-artists.

People like that are hard to persuade.

However, though small in number, they're good to have around because they force constant re-examination of the actual realities among all the virtual substitutes.

Consequently, one of the things I'm always on the look-out for is examples of cutting-edge presentation of Web information. I don't want to know what's cool; I want to know what's out there that would make people want to buy.

A "must" stop on the Web for more than a year has been Studeo.com, the Website of a Provo, UT-based advertising agency which also happens to be the employer of Randall Whitted, brilliant and opinionated contributor to CMP Media's TechWeb News, the online email newsletter.

Studeo.com's Website has an opening screen that looks like a movie intro; inside little light bulbs brighten as a small electrical impulses run down the wire. Clients include majors such as American Express, Marriott and Novell but what you need to see is something labeled "Just for Fun."

VW's "Turbonium" Molecule

Be patient while the graphics build on your page. Once it's loaded you'll have a virtual music synthesizer on your computer. You can play basic notes from an online keyboard, clang cymbals, beat drums and set background rhythms going in Techno, Pop, Jazz, Funk, Disco or Samba. The truly gifted can probably create new music although techno-duffers like me are more likely to create new definitions for the word "cacophony."

... this is just a "taste" of what's coming to your ears as your fingers poke into the Web of the future.

Useful? I don't know but this is just a "taste" of what's coming to your ears as your fingers poke into the Web of the future.

If you want to see what's coming visually, go to "Solemates: The Century in Shoes."

This handsome site, developed by San Francisco advertising agency The Marketing Store, demonstrates how the Web is migrating towards television. Watch those shoes revolving on your screen and you'll understand how full action video will transform the Web.

Solemates is both entertaining and educational. It's got sound, videos, graphics, motion, interactivity. It's compelling. Be warned that this site requires you to download both the QuickTime and Macromedia Flash plug-ins for your browser but don't worry: they're free, and installation, though it takes five or ten minutes, is fairly painless.

Once you've got the two plug-ins, take a tour of some of the other premiere Websites that are leading the way toward the fully-connected, interactive future.

Try Volkswagen's "Turbonium" site built around its clever advertising campaign for the new VW Beetle Turbo. See speeding Beetles zoom across your screen, materialize from screen pixels and then rocket off the elemental charts while you download the Ben Neill music from the Turbonium commercial. Neat.

Prefer good old American fare? Try Ford's "Better Ideas" site. But be prepared. It's not your old-fashioned Ford anymore. The new Ford Motor Company includes Volvo, Jaguar, Aston-Martin and Mazda as well as the home-grown Mercury and Lincoln divisions. Words fade, flip, dissolve and dance on your screen. Impressive.

Want to see what the Japanese are doing? Visit Yugo Nakamura's extraordinary Typospace Website which offers a deeply philosophical look at existential typography. Say What? Well, it's a game based on the typewriter keyboard. You type and the letters spin up, float and settle on the screen. Mesmerizing.

All of these sites represent state of the art innovation by aggressive competitors. They're setting a pace that won't let up.

The question for any business that wants to stay in business is no longer whether the Internet is a fad but rather, "How do I get that for my Website?"

Tech Web (http://www.techweb.com/)
Studeo.com (http://www.studeo.com/)
Just for Fun (http://www.studeo.com/flash/index.html)
Solemates (http://www.centuryinshoes.com/)
Turbonium (http://www.turbonium.com/flash/index.html)
Ford Motor Company (http://www2.ford.com)
Typospace (http://www.yugop.com/typospace.html#)

All of these sites represent state of the art innovation by aggressive competitors. They're setting a pace that won't let up.

Successful Online Commerce Is Simple

If you are trying to sell things online, you have a number of immediate challenges—in case you didn't know. The solutions are all simple.

Among the biggest challenges is letting people know you are out there. Another is making sure that once they've found you, they like your site. A third is — once they've found you and liked your site — creating the desire to buy something from you. Finally, you need to do your best to make that purchase easy, secure and satisfying.

You have some serious competition out there. The big guys are online, of course, and some of their sites are spectacular.

The miracle of the Net, though, is that little guys with a little know-how can make just as big a splash as the biggies. A multi-state, multi-outlet shop and a mom & pop specialty store are equal in the eyes of the Web surfer. Both have about the same chance to make a first impression. The software is out there to create bells and whistles or a clean and spare shopping experience, and anyone with the time and the inclination to learn can master it.

Visit Yahoo!'s How-To resources for links to a number of useful tutorials on HTML and Web Design.

Design skills, of course, are not as easy to master, but don't be downcast. The other side of that coin is that some skilled designers don't quite understand the Web or the ordinary person's Internet experience.

Their work is gorgeous, but they work in ivory towers of fast Internet connections and super speed computers with nice large-screened monitors and all the plug-ins. Their previous work experience may have involved total control of the colors, sizes, type faces, paper, and presentation of their work. This isn't always possible on the Internet.

Spectacular animation, small windows that open up, neat little sounds and other cool tricks can so slow down the visitor's machine that he or she gets frustrated and leaves before seeing the full show.

A reasonably sophisticated visitor can turn down the music, turn off the graphics, and change the color of both the text and background.

A page that looks wonderful on a big monitor might require the visitor to scroll up and down

The miracle of the Net, though, is that little guys with a little know-how can make just as big a splash as the biggies.

to see it on a small one. The visitor might choose not to — or not know to — and miss your name, address or other key information unless it's prominently placed near the top.

So, keep it simple, sweetheart, and you can't go far wrong.

A great ordering system is worth a half dozen neat design tricks. If you are paying someone else to design an Internet storefront for you, make sure they concentrate on an order form that's secure and easy to find and use.

Back to the number one challenge: once you've got a site, how are they going to find you?

There are a number of ways— a lot depends on your target market. Are you going to sell to the whole world, or do you want a market in your own geographical area? Either way, you can't depend on Web surfers to find you via a search engine — though you should visit them all and submit your site.

Don't overlook the old fashioned ways of publicizing your Web presence. Make sure it's in all your ads, if you have any. Put it on your stationery and business cards and print it on your packaging.

Finally, try to get other people to review your site and send customers your way. An example of what I'm talking about is the BizRate Guide, a free, independent listing of Web shops. Merchants apply to be listed, and when their application is accepted, their site is reviewed and included.

BizRate Guide was created as a free service by Binary Compass Enterprises, a business that measures customer satisfaction on the Web and provides standardized information to merchants. Whether you are shopping or selling, you owe yourself a look at it.

Yahoo! How-To resources, Web Design, etc. (http://howto.yahoo.com/resources/html_guides)
How to suggest a site to Yahoo! (http://www.yahoo.com/info/suggest/)
AltaVista Help—Add a page to(http://www.altavista.com/av/content/addurl.htm)
WebCrawler Help: Add URL (http://www.WebCrawler.com/Help/GetListed/AddURLS.html)
BizRate (http://www.bizrate.com)
Apply to the BizRate Program (http://www.bizrate.com/MerchantOnly/merchant_terms.html)
Binary Compass Enterprises (http://www.binarycompass.com/)

Back to the number one challenge: once you've got a site, how are they going to find you?

Competition Drives Office Supply Prices Down

One of the major promises of Internet commerce is that it will drive prices down as consumers are able to compare prices globally rather than locally.

Consider the exploding online market for office supplies. All the major mega-stores now offer their wares over the Internet. Their prices are posted online and anyone can check and compare before making the buying decision.

This open pricing has created fierce competition that puts the buyer in control at the moment, but how long it will continue is anyone's guess. If you're in charge of buying your company's office supplies stock up now while you've got the upper hand.

For instance, Staples offers free shipping on any purchase over $50 and guarantees it will match any other office supply company's price. OfficeMax and Office Depot have met Staples' Free-Shipping-Over-$50 standard but they're offering an incredible 155% "Low Price Guarantee." If you can find the same item offered for less they'll meet the price and then discount it by an additional 55%. Now that's competition.

An offer like that would make you think the big bricks-and-mortar companies are all confident they're offering rock-bottom, unbeatable prices but are they?

A recent online check on pricing for laserwriter toner cartridges was very instructive.

Laserwriters which came onto the market 15 years ago at a cost of about $8,000 have now fallen in price to about $300 and are found in almost every office. However, their toner cartridge prices have remained fairly constant at about $100 each. It's evident now the profit center has shifted to the supplies side and a business will now spend much more on toner than it will on the printer itself during the normal product life.

We searched for a Hewlett Packard 5MP Laserwriter cartridge and found the regular list price at $109. Office Depot offered it at $89.99; Staples listed it at $89.21, and OfficeMax had it for $69.99.

Two online-only office supply vendors had comparable spreads: AtYourOffice quoted it at $74.95. Onlineofficesupplies beat everyone with a price of $64.29.

AtYourOffice includes free shipping on any order over $25. Onlineofficesupplies charges a

If you're in charge of buying your company's office supplies, stock up now while you've got the upper hand.

flat 5% for shipping any order except in Maryland or Virginia where sales tax is levied instead. Still, their price with 5% added was $2.50 below the OfficeMax price.

A comparison on another toner cartridge showed prices ranging from $64.34 down to $53.99 — this time the low price leader was OfficeMax, beating out Onlineofficesupplies by 70 cents. The advantage of using the Internet, however, is reduced if you have to invest vast amounts of your time to sort out all these prices. Wouldn't it be great if someone did it for us?

It is great and they are doing it for us.

BuyersZone of Watertown, MA offers a matching service for businesses and suppliers. You enter your ZIP Code and the product you want, they return a list of nearby vendors with an online form seeking price quotes. If you're in a part of the country where they don't have any local sources you can go to e-Catalog Central which has combined some of the largest vendors' online offerings. Unfortunately it's slow and results organized by price often don't reveal any of the necessary details you need to figure out what's being quoted.

A much more promising comparison shopper is mySimon, based in Santa Clara, CA, which uses proprietary technology to search more than 1,000 online merchants in categories such as Computers, Books & Music, Electronics, Fashion, Flowers — even office products.

Choose Office Supplies as the category, Cartridge, Toner and Ribbon as the section, enter your printer model and the results come back ranging in price from $74.96 to $63.07 for the same Hewlett Packard cartridge we so laboriously tracked through all those individual Web-sites.

Once you've got the lowest price you click to buy and are automatically switched to the Online vendor's Wesbite where your order is ready to be processed.

Staples (http://www. staples.com)
OfficeMax (http://www.officemax.com)
Office Depot (http://www.officedepot.com)
AtYourOffice (http://www.atyouroffice.com)
Onlineofficesupplies (http://www.onlineofficesupplies.com)
BuyersZone (http://www.buyerszone.com)
mySimon (http://www.mySimon.com)

A much more promising comparison shopper is mySimon...

E-Banking Online Offers Some Consolations

Banking has changed fundamentally over the past few decades. Once, whether our balances were fat or slim, we expected to know the people at our local bank and we expected them to know us.

Today, multi-state banking and the Internet has made the whole business both more difficult and more convenient.

When I was growing up our local bank had two branches, one in the county seat, the other in a town about ten miles away. Sometime afterwards they opened a third branch with a drive-up window.

Things changed and got more official, as they had to. I moved to another county and the local bank was a cousin of the one I'd known as a child.

Then a multi-county bank took over those banks. Local names gave way to a more generic one. Decisions weren't made locally, but we still knew our local bankers and tellers, and they knew us. (We could still check our balances or move money from savings to checking simply by telephoning and relying on the fact that June or Peggy or Lois or Rosemary recognized our voices.)

That kind of banking was very reassuring.

Then, when a multi-state megabank took over, and we felt as if Godzilla had moved in. All the tellers were shuffled about, and suddenly we were being asked for photo ID at branches where we'd banked for nearly two decades. The bank officer we knew best left the organization. Soon his assistants had gone too.

Decisions were made in another city, in another state. Mistakes were made and accounts frozen inadvertently. Account numbers were changed. We were unhappy.

If it hadn't been for the Internet, I, for one, would have been sorely tempted to pull my money out and stuff it into my mattress.

The new bank offered online banking, and I was intrigued. Soon, I was hooked.

I can check my balances online, find out whether checks have cleared, pay bills, transfer money between accounts. If I wanted to, I could monitor and manage my investments online. I

... multi-state banking and the Internet has made the whole business both more difficult and more convenient.

can export the information to my Quicken program so I can keep track of my finances. Whether it's in the middle of the night or during a free quarter-hour between appointments, I can bank whenever I find the time.

Although the bank's software seems a little slow, it has improved even in the few months since I've used it.

Progress giveth and progress taketh away. Sometimes it's a wash.

Many banks offer similar account access and management online. Demonstrations and tutorials are available and generally easy to use and understand. If your bank offers online banking and investments, you will find information about it at their Website. Don't be timid about exploring it.

Cleveland-based KeyCorp's KeyBank is pushing online banking as the awkwardly named Key2Your$+Internet. This company offers instant access to transactions, unlike most, including mine, that batch transactions and download them at intervals of a day or more. Key's electronic commerce head, Patrick J. Swanick, explained that the bank's "customers and small businesses can now organize their finances on their computers."

There's a demo at the site that's easy to find, and simple to use and understand. It will give you a taste of what's available.

You have to drill down several layers from North Carolina-based Wachovia Bank's main Website to find their online banking demo, but the software is almost identical to KeyBank's.

For more information on online banking, My Virtual Reference Desk has a huge selection of online banking and investment links. Several of them list Internet addresses and email addresses for worldwide banks. Remember information on them may be out of date — I saw a couple of banks listed as not offering the service, when I know they do. Go to the bank's own Website to do your research.

Wachovia PC Access (http://www.wachovia.com/pcaccess/index.html)
KeyBank (http://www.key.com/)
MVRD Investment and Online Banking Resources (http://www.refdesk.com/online.html)

There's a demo at the site that's easy to find, and simple to use and understand. It will give you a taste of what's available.

Online Auctions Are Growing Attractions

Among the billions of dollars being flung at e-commerce sites by big investors and venture capitalists is a small but steady stream of greenbacks slapping from pocket to pocket among the small fry who are learning to buy and sell online, one item at a time.

Once you've tried the online auction experience you begin to understand some of the real underlying power of e-commerce and why the Internet really is fundamentally altering the world economy.

There are reportedly now more than a thousand individual auction sites on the Web and the largest, eBay, boasts more than a million on-going auctions a day in more than a thousand categories.

People have always been willing to buy and sell almost anything eyeball-to-eyeball and the proliferation of Web auctions proves people will do it screen-to-screen as well. The difference between a country auction and the online experience is that variety and selection are vastly greater.

If you're looking for something specific you need only type the word into the search engine. The computer's dumb efficiency is at your service.

But it is in the similarities rather than the differences that e-commerce is blooming. According to Auction Tribune, a Website devoted to online auctions, San Francisco-based eBay rates number one among the top ten for both on-site resources and relationship services; it ranks second behind OnSale for ease of use, and second behind DealDeal for customer confidence.

Confidence is the essential ingredient. Buyers and sellers both need to feel secure, protected and reassured there's a larger community interest in fair play that will protect smaller individuals in their transactions.

This is one of eBay's great strengths. Buyers and sellers must register at the site before participating in any auction and agree to simple but comprehensive rules of conduct.

There are extensive explanations and guidelines, even community chat groups where you can talk to others. There's also plenty of feedback everywhere you turn, including a star rating system for both buyers and sellers based on previous activity. Everyone is encouraged to rate

The computer's dumb efficiency is at your service.

the quality of the transaction experience and all those comments (positive and negative) can be seen on the eBay member's profile.

This is the sort of self-policing that an open Internet makes possible. Let the Buyer Beware is still the rule of the market but the computerized world makes it mighty hard for a scoundrel to stay in business.

Smart. Deals. Online.™

Fees are only charged to sellers, not buyers. There is a nominal "Insertion Fee" to list an item for sale that ranges from a quarter to two dollars. A "Final Value" fee is assessed on the winning bid: 5% of the first $25, 2 1/2% up to $1,000 and 1 1/4% above that. Total fees charged to a seller are less than 4% for a $100 item.

When you place items to be auctioned, eBay keeps a computerized tally of your sales and their fees. Once your bill reaches $10 you must pay up or your selling rights are suspended. If you're a regular seller you can provide eBay a credit card number and they'll deduct the fees as they occur.

When you bid on items as a buyer you can enter a single bid at the minimum and wait for others to bid against you or you can enter a maximum bid and let the computer enter "Proxy Bids" on your behalf up to your maximum.

If someone does bid over your maximum eBay sends you a "Heads-Up" email in case you want to reconsider and re-bid.

I don't know about others but when I got a recent heads-up I certainly reconsidered and re-bid. Then as the hours dwindled to minutes and minutes dissolved into seconds I stayed glued to the computer, finally clicking the reload button every few seconds to see if anyone might outbid me at the last moment.

It was a horse race. It was neck and neck. It was going, going, gone! And it was mine.

eBay (http://www.ebay.com)
Auction Tribune (http://auctiontribune.com)
OnSale (http://onsale.com)
DealDeal (http://dealdeal.com/)

If someone does bid over your maximum eBay sends you a "Heads-Up" email in case you want to reconsider and re-bid.

Online Shopping Extends Catalog Reach

Increasingly I find myself relying on the Internet for my mail-order purchases.

I'm a committed catalog shopper. Although I go into malls from time to time, I love mail-order shopping best.

The number of catalogs I get in the mail attests to that. Once a company has identified a "live one" like me, they go into overdrive. By September, the flow deepens and widens into a flood.

Catalogs are piled on every surface, pages marked with little colored flags. I've found perfect Christmas presents for my husband, children, siblings, in-laws, nieces, nephews, and friends. I even have ideas about birthdays, anniversaries and other celebrations.

If, as they say, "it's the thought that counts," all the people on my list should feel well taken care of.

Catalogs, though, have a habit of straying. They slip behind bureaus, under chairs, into trash cans—out of sight, out of mind. I lose track of what I meant to buy.

Increasingly I find myself relying on the Internet for my mail-order purchases.

Many mail-order companies have Internet outposts.

One of the biggest — the amazing Amazon.com — began to get much of my business because they made shopping for books so easy, and almost everyone I know loves books.

Amazon.com has never loaded down my bedside table with printed catalogs — they started out selling online. Other companies have begun to study Amazon to learn how to do it.

Amazon.com offers recommendations based on your previous purchases (and what people who bought the same book you did also bought). They gift wrap and send books out promptly. They keep track of your shopping list between visits so you can think about whether you really want that book or not. They'll even look for out-of-print books for you.

Venerable L.L. Bean of Maine, granddaddy of the catalog industry, has an intricate and interesting site, where you can order online from your printed catalog or browse a limited selection of wares.

Lands' End also has a Website to complement their many catalogs. It's cozy, comforting and easy to use. They have stories from the catalog and a constantly updated "overstocks" section of discounted clothes.

The best part of it is the Intelligent Order Blank. If you're like me you may have a stack of dog-eared catalogs from the various Lands' End enterprises, offering household linens, children's clothes, career woman office clothes, luggage, "et cetera, et cetera" (to quote Yul Brynner as the King of Siam).

With the Intelligent Order Blank, you can consolidate your order in a single Internet experience. Place your stack on the desk next to your PC, go through the catalogs one at a time, enter each item number into the IOB, get a confirmation that what you want is available, and, when you're all done, click your order on its electronic way. I like that.

If you want to send food, you have endless choices. Almost all offer a choice between online and phone ordering, depending on your comfort level.

The Flying Noodle from Vermont, offers a wild variety of pastas, sauces and olive oils individually or in combinations. You can even sign up for the Flying Noodle's Pasta Club! Mangia, Mangia! Their secure online order forms are quick and easy to use.

The Oregon Cupboard has truffle cakes, smoked salmon, candy, preserves and honey from "artisans" in Oregon. They, too, have easy to use online order forms, or you can phone in your order.

I've also had good luck ordering from Twin Peaks Gourmet Trading Post which sells everything from sauces to pies to live Maine Lobsters to a Celebration cake packed in dry ice along with plates, forks, napkins, candles and so on.

The Abbey of Gethsemani in Kentucky sells cheese, fruitcake and bourbon fudge made by the monks. I guess the monks don't choose to hang around waiting for email orders, though. Once you've decided what you want you must print out the order form, fill it in by hand, and send it by fax or snailmail.

This is only the tip of the iceberg.

Amazon.com (http://www.amazon.com)
L.L. Bean (http://www.llbean.com/)
Lands' End (http://www.landsend.com)
Abbey of Gethsemani (http://www.monks.org/)
Flying Noodle (http://www.flyingnoodle.com)
Oregon Cupboard (http://www.oregoncupboard.com/)
Twin Peaks Gourmet Trading Post (http://tpeaks.com/)

This is only the tip of the iceberg.

Online Grocery Shopping Is Growing & Ripening

Forty or fifty years ago, grandmother telephoned in a daily grocery order to a neighborhood market. It was delivered to her kitchen door later the same day. She was billed monthly.

It was fairly common in those days. It was called progress.

Cars, suburbia and "super" markets put an end to it. That was also called progress.

With the advent of the Internet, home grocery delivery is returning and it may again be called progress.

Three years ago, when Microsoft Emperor Bill Gates predicted that by 2005 a third of all food sales would be handled electronically, skeptics laughed.

The road ahead just didn't seem that smooth. Bound to be bumps, lots of obstacles to overcome. The $400 billion a year grocery industry, based on fresh produce and perishables just didn't seem a likely candidate for Internet competition.

That was then. This is now. When the 800-lb e-commerce-Gorilla Amazon.com announced it had paid $42.5 million for a 35% stake in HomeGrocer.com it became necessary for industry skeptics to shake their brains free of musty old ideas that no longer compute.

HomeGrocer.com, began in 1998 in Seattle, WA. The day after the Amazon.com announcement they expanded their service to Portland, OR. California is next. They plan to be operating in a dozen cities by the turn of the century but at the moment their staff is small enough to list by name on their Website.

HomeGrocer offers over 11,000 items, including fresh produce, milk, meat and fish. Delivery for orders of more than $75 is free. If you order before 11 pm you get next-day delivery to your kitchen counter from one of the company's custom-designed refrigerated trucks. Customer satisfaction is guaranteed.

At the moment they don't accept coupons but competition may change that.

Competition? Yes, this is not just a Northwest fad. Online grocery shopping, after a slow start, is beginning to build a real following in major metropolitan markets across the continent.

In the Northeast, for instance, "Peapod" of Skokie, IL which launched its service in 1989, and

... it became necessary for industry skeptics to shake their brains free of musty old ideas that no longer compute.

Hannaford Grocery's "HomeRuns" compete in the same suburban markets around Boston. Both have their own fleet of vans and offer free delivery for orders of more than $60. Both accept coupons.

Shoplink, based in Westwood, MA, is also battling for customers around Beantown and offers its own proprietary software on CD-ROM. In addition to groceries you can order special services like dry cleaning, video rental, shoe repair and film processing. They'll even install their own refrigerator in your garage or basement and deliver to the fridge while you're away from home.

NetGrocer of North Brunswick, NJ, which was one of the first to offer online grocery shopping, doesn't restrict its market area. They ship by FedEx anywhere in the country.

In Canada, The PeachTree Network has affiliated with grocery stores in major markets to offer online ordering and home delivery in St. John's, Toronto, North Bay, Winnipeg, Edmonton, and Vancouver. They're planning to expand further in Canada but also in San Francisco, Oklahoma City and Chicago.

Big cities aren't the only markets experiencing the online rush. Many smaller and independent stores have affiliated with the Minneapolis-based Grocery Shopping Network. They list hundreds of online grocery stores by state, many of whom have only rudimentary Websites that may offer only coupons at the moment. But some are experimenting with online ordering.

For example, Jerry's Foods of Sanibel, FL offers an online form that you can print out and fax to them after typing in your grocery needs. They'll deliver it 72 hours later for a $20 fee.

It may not seem that high-tech but I'll bet that Jerry will be a couple of leaps ahead of the competition when ordering groceries "online" becomes as common as it was when grandmother used the telephone line.

HomeGrocer.com (http://www.homegrocer.com)
Peapod (http://www.peapod.com/)
Homeruns (http://www.homeruns.com/)
Shoplink (http://www.shoplink.com/)
NetGrocer (http://www.netgrocer.com/)
The PeachTree Network (http://www.thepeachtree.net)
Grocery Shopping Network (http://grocerywebsites.com/)
Jerry's Foods (http://www.jerrysfoods.com/faxmail.htm)

Big cities aren't the only markets experiencing the online rush.

Amazon.com Launches Widespread Retail Attack

A classic Farside cartoon by Gary Larsen of more than a decade ago portrayed a group of settlers surrounded by attacking Indians with flames coming from one of the circled wagons. "They're using flaming arrows," says one befuddled defender, "Are they allowed to do that?"

The image came to mind following the 1999 mid-summer announcement by Amazon.com that it had launched two new "stores to sell electronic equipment and toys;" it also acquired a major stake in Gear.com, an online retailer of sports equipment.

Earlier in the year Amazon bought major shares in HomeGrocer.com, an online grocery store that offers home delivery, Pets.com, a supplier of pet supplies and pet information, and Drugstore.com, a major online seller of prescription drugs. It also owns PlanetAll, a Web-based address book and calendar service, Internet Movie Database, a comprehensive resource on more than 150,000 movies made since 1892, and LiveBid, an online auction company.

At the close of the year it opened "stores" for Video Games, Software and Hardware — literally the hammer and nails stuff found in Home Improvement stores.

Amazon.com, was launched in Seattle, WA in July 1995 as "the world's largest bookstore" — something of a stretch since it didn't have a physical store and most of its inventory consisted of a computerized database that tapped into the warehouses of traditional wholesalers.

What it did have was a vision based on an understanding of the true power of the Internet, a strategy of steep discounting, an amazing amount of cash and a more amazing willingness to lose money to build the business. Amazon has yet to earn a profit after four years of operations but the stock market values it in billions.

A lot of small independent bookstores couldn't compete with the steep discounts that Amazon offered — usually 30% — and many closed their doors. Even some big bookstores, most noticeably Barnes and Noble which for years had itself been putting the squeeze on the independents, cried foul over Amazon's claim to offer more books. When Amazon bumped its discount on New York Times Bestsellers up to 50%, B&N followed suit.

Consumers were the immediate beneficiaries but small (and even large) independents who had to abandon profits on their most popular titles began asking "Is that fair?"

Fair, as many wise parents have taught their children, is a four-letter word that oughtn't be mentioned in polite company.

small independents ... began asking "Is that fair?"

Amazon's latest move finally removes the veil that has been obscuring people's view of the leading (and still money-losing) e-commerce retailer. Dropping the façade of intellectual book-seller, Amazon founder Jeff Bezos has put on the war bonnet, daubed himself in paint and declared that his goal is to become the world's leading online department store. The new corporate slogan boasts that Amazon offers "Earth's Biggest Selection" of products.

This is a change that should be rocking the seismographs in businesses around the globe. Amazon logged its 12 millionth individual customerin late 1999. It keeps adding new customers and new product lines.

Don't worry about the impact on your local bookstore or drugstore or toystore or sports store. Start thinking about the impact this is going to have on your local Wal-Mart.

Commerce, which is the foundation of culture, is going through a revolution and no business will be immune from the changes.

As Americans and their shopping moved to the 'burbs after World War II, the mall became the defining element of the late 20th century's social compact. The symbolic multi-floored department stores that once anchored downtown commercial centers and gave cities their vitality were almost universally abandoned in decaying urban cores.

Suddenly, a convergence of technologies is threatening the malls with selection, price and service that will be hard to beat — ask any independent bookstore. Amazon may be the first to use the flaming arrows but it won't be the last.

The quality-of-life-issue facing environmental activists in the next decade won't be the growing threat of suburban sprawl and Mall culture. It will more likely be the very serious question of where to put the huge warehouses and distribution centers for the FedEx, UPS, RPS and USPS delivery vehicles that are becoming a more and more prevalent part of our daily traffic.

Amazon.com (http://www.amazon.com)
HomeGrocer.com (http://www.homegrocer.com)
Pets.com (http://www.pets.com)
Drugstore.com (http://www.drugstore.com)
PlanetAll (http://www.planetall.com)
Internet Movie Database (http://www.imdb.com)
LiveBid (http://www.livebid.com)

Amazon may be the first to use the flaming arrows but it won't be the last.

Online Commerce Increases Credit Card Values

Got a credit card? Got a debit card? Charge card? Smart card? Cash card? Phone card?

Feel like you're naked when you leave home without one? Feel empowered when you put one down to cover your purchases? Feel vaguely nauseated when it comes time to pay the bills at the end of the month?

If you don't like credit card bills you can switch to a debit card which offers the convenience of sucking funds from your account instantly when you make a purchase instead of waiting for you to go through the end of the month anxiety attacks.

The debit card's "convenience" however, has reportedly left some card users so thoroughly confused about their current account balances they've fallen back on BOE ledger-keeping (back-of-envelope scribbling). Others resort to daily telephoning to "1-800-Call-My-Bank" — a process that drives costs up for the card issuers.

In the last quarter of the 20th century the little plastic "charge-a-cards" have become such a fixture of American consumerism that card marketers now fight for consumers' SOW — Share of Wallet — and the emergence of online commerce has only accelerated the process.

In fact, the virtual reality of online commerce is beginning to bend even a banker's imagination. It's now possible to apply for a credit card online and 30 seconds later be ordering merchandise online that is charged to the card you didn't even have a minute before.

In February, 1998 NextCard introduced the first Internet VISA card where consumers can apply for a credit card online and be approved in 30 seconds. After approval the new virtual card holder can work the upgrades and earn rewards that include airline miles and merchandise rebates for purchases both online and off. Amazon.com thought enough of their operation to buy a 10% stake in late '99.

Every card offers special opportunities. Some offer no annual fees. Others offer special low introductory rates that later jump as if propelled from a trampoline.

What savvy consumers really need to know is what's available now and how it compares to what they already have.

... card marketers now fight for consumers' SOW — Share of Wallet

Enter CardWeb of Gettysburg, PA which was launched in April, 1998 providing information to both consumers and providers of card services. This is the place to come if you're looking for your first credit card or your last. You'll certainly get the low-down on how your current card stacks up against the marketplace.

Check the CardTrak service to compare current interest rates and fees. You'll be surprised at the range of offers available, many of which are hyper-linked for immediate online contact.

For example, in mid-'99, First USA Bank of Dela-ware offered a 5.9% interest rate with no annual fee. By contrast Wachovia Bank in Georgia offered an 8.5% interest rate with a $98 annual fee.

If you were looking for a card that gave something back for each of your purchases Dividend Miles VISA in Georgia offered a card with an 18.4% interest rate and a $70 annual fee — naturally you earn airline miles for each dollar charged so the higher interest rate and annual fee might be worth it to you if that's your goal.

If you're looking for a high credit limit ($5,000 to $100,000) Card Search Online provides a whole slew of Platinum cards with interest rates ranging from 9.9% to 18.4%. (There are no nickel-and-diming annual fees if you have that kind of limit, thank you; pass the Grey Poupon, please.)

CardWeb always lists its "featured" card issuers first, generally those who offer their cards nationwide, and all of them include links to their individual Websites. However, other issuers include 800 numbers so you can call and apply.

If you're a thorough-going card junkie you might want to wander over to the card provider side where you can learn more than you ever wanted to know about who makes cards, who supplies ATM machines, who sells mailing lists for good prospects ... just how important a SOW can be online.

NextCard (http://www.nextcard.com)
CardWeb (http://www.cardweb.com)

This is the place to come if you're looking for your first credit card or your last.

Promote Your Online Presence

Your business card says it all: name, title, business, address, phone, fax, pager, email, Website... You gotta a Website? Cool! You gotcherown dot-com? Cool! You do e-commerce? Way cool!

But beyond your humble workhorse business-card (which now has as much information crammed onto it as a formal entry in a medical dictionary) how do you differentiate yourself and your enterprise from the millions of others online all clamoring for attention and business?

Go online, you're told, and you can market to the world.

Of course it does take a little bit of techno-savvy to get the code written and the Website up and the search engines notified but, hey, anyone with a pony-tail, a large pizza and an all-nighter can do that for you, right?

Well, almost anyone.

Once up, though, the success of your Website and the potential for any sort of e-commerce depends on old-fashioned promotion. People still have to know who you are, where you are, what you're selling, why it's desirable and how to order. They also have to feel comfortable with you.

We're talking image. There's a smell to success and an odor to failure. How do you tip the olfactory senses in your favor?

One of the best ways is through the judicious use of promotional items that project an image of a company many times your size.

You've seen them before: pens, pencils, matchbooks, cups, caps ... anything that can be imprinted with your company's name and logo. They're a step above your calling card because they offer some benefit or utility that will keep your name in front of the potential customer on a regular basis.

There's a smell to success and an odor to failure. How do you tip the olfactory senses in your favor?

They can cost anywhere from pennies to hundreds of dollars depending on your budget and the impression you're trying to create.

So how do you find what you're looking for? Go online, of course.

The Internet makes all this information available and there's a lot of it.

Start at Logomall's Promotional Products Reference Guide where you can read about famously successful promotional items such as the 1881 logo-imprinted bookbag, the 1893 H.J.

Heinz pickle charm, or the wooden pencils dropped over the Philippines during WW II bearing General Douglas MacArthur's words "I shall return."

Imprint Magazine's devoted an online editorial to explain the industry's view on once-in-a-lifetime promotional opportunities offered by the millennium.

If you'd rather cut straight to the chase you can, naturally, search among their 45,000 promotional products by name, category, delivery time and price range.

Don't imagine that this is the only game in town though. Plenty of companies offer name and logo imprinting on specialty products.

Opening a Bed & Breakfast and want to look a little more corporate? Visit Promotional Media and look at what's known in the trade as "Hotel Amenities." Yes, you too can have your own logo on that little bar of soap and shower cap.

Marketing a brand new time-saving device? Go to PromoCity and check out their quartz watches with custom designed logos on the face.

Looking for the ever-popular coffee mug with your name and logo on it? Look at The Competitive Edge from Des Moines which offers everything from plain white porcelain to stainless steel commuter mugs and even gourmet coffee packs.

Thinking more upscale and want to outfit your whole staff with handsome polo shirts with embroidered logos for your next sales show? Look at Lands' End and L.L. Bean online catalogs. Both have corporate sales departments and just about anything these giant catalog retailers offer can be embroidered, embossed or screen-printed to promote your business.

You gotcherown dot-com? Cool. Now tell your customers how to find it when they go online.

Logomall's Promotional Products Reference Guide (http://www.logomall.com/about/APP1.HTM)
Imprint Magazine's online editorial
        (http://www.logomall.com/imprintPM/issues/Winter-1998/editorial.htm)
Promotional Media (http://www.promotionalmedia.com/hotel.html)
PromoCity (http://www.promocity.com/premiums.htm)
The Competitve Edge (http://www.compet.com/coffeemugs.html)
Lands' End Corporate Sales (http://www.landsend.com/corpsales/)
L.L. Bean Corporate Sales (http://www.llbean.com/corporateSales/index.noframes.html)

You gotcherown dot-com? Cool. Now tell your customers ...

"Entrepreneur's Mind" Offers Insights

If there were ever need for compelling evidence that "Content is king," the newsy feature-zine "Entrepreneur's Mind" is proof enough.

EM presents itself as a Web resource devoted to entrepreneurial essays from experts who've been there and done that. Anyone who's struggling with all the many hats an entrepreneur must wear will appreciate the advice and warm to the war stories.

Read about Keynote Entrepreneur Pete Slosberg, of Pete's Wicked Ale, who:

• took up beer brewing only after finding out how long it took for wine to ferment

• decided to launch his own business based on three major criteria ... and then decided to brew beer

• almost lost his entire business in its infancy when his contract brewer shut its doors in Chapter 7 bankruptcy, giving him and 15 friends two and half days to bottle and remove all the beer they had on premises

• attributes his success to having "great people busting their buns."

Visit the Expert's Corner and learn about what academic Jeffrey Shuman calls "The Rhythm of Business" which entrepreneurs use to:

• launch the process "which will manifest itself at various times as different business configurations"

• satisfy their customers rather than beat out the competition

...entrepreneurial essays from experts who've been there and done that.

Examine the Launch Pad where Armando Conti's efforts to create the "premier domestic espresso machine" are described. And consider this: the "Espresso Armando" coffee machine actually owes its inspiration to his inability to find a good second-hand espresso maker for his own home use. His frustration at not being able to make a really good cup of coffee on a consistent basis led him to make a brand new machine — and launch a business.

Go to Global Perspective for a report on Finnish companies doing businesses with Russian startups. Stop by Arthur Andersen for their report on Cybertaxation.

Scan the Archives for previous essays on entrepreneurial ventures like HandsOnToys, Nantucket Nectars and Mecklermedia.

For instance, any struggling entrepreneur will empathize with Alan Meckler's experience in 1992, after years of worrying about meeting payroll, being ready to throw in the towel and then listening to Mitch Kapor, founder of Lotus Development Corp, speak at a trade show that Meckler had organized.

"It was like going to see Billy Graham or some evangelist and being converted," Meckler says." I was there and I had lost faith and he put me back over the top." (Mecklermedia has since gone public, organizes Internet trade shows in 26 countries, publishes Internet World magazine and maintains the "iWorld" Website which attracts more than half a million viewers a month.)

Although Entrepreneur's Mind is highly-informative and loaded with well-written essays on entrepreneurial topics, this is one of those sites that might be puzzling to a traditional revenue-based business operator.

EM seems to have no financial grounding in anything other than the early Internet's "gift-based economy." Everything here is given away free. It's an ongoing treat for us but what gives?

Created by The Benlore Company of Watertown, MA, EM must be viewed as an example of Benlore's own wares: the display cake put in the bakery window.

Benlore provides Web development, consulting, analysis and research. They focus on entrepreneurial ventures because that's the kind of client they want (and understand).

Obviously it's an entrepreneurial ploy on their part. One that might be working — or in the process of transforming to meet customers' needs.

Entrepreneur's Mind (http://www.benlore.com/index2.html)
Keynote Entrepreneur (http://www.benlore.com/files/emkey2_1.html)
Experts Corner (http://www.benlore.com/files/emexpert2_1.html)
Launch Pad (http://www.benlore.com/files/emlaunch2_1.html)
Global Perspective (http://www.benlore.com/files/emglobal2_1.html)
Archives (http://www.benlore.com/files/archive.html)

"I was there and I had lost faith and he put me back over the top."

Take the Test Before Striking Out

Maybe this is the year: the break-out year, the year you actually tell the boss to take your job and stuff it, the year you find out for certain whether the business idea that wakes you at 3 a.m. is actually your life's dream yearning to be born or a nightmare waiting to happen.

Before you abandon the monotony of picking up your regular paycheck for the excitement of trying to issue a regular payroll you may want to consider whether you have what it takes to be a successful entrepreneur.

Naturally there a lot of different things needed for different businesses but there are characteristics that are helpful in all, some traits that are indispensable.

Want a simple test to find out? Take the Entrepreneur Test offered by Small Business Knowledge Base, an Israeli Website created by Meir Liraz.

Answering 10 simple questions by clicking on suggested answers will give you a numerical score that ranges from Excellent ("You are a born entrepreneur. If you are not presently running your own business you should definitely start one — the sooner the better. You are on your way to fame and riches.") to Unsatisfactory ("Forget your dreams of being your own boss, it's not for you. You'd better keep your comfortable and secure job. Why bother with all the risks and hustles of starting a business?")

... you may want to consider whether you have what it takes to be a successful entrepreneur.

Naturally an online quiz like this can't be definitive but Liraz goes on to point out that characteristics that appear most frequently in successful managers include drive, thinking ability (both analytical and creative), competency in human relations, communications skills, and technical knowledge.

If you're looking for technical knowledge Liraz's site is a good place to start, particularly if you're just starting to explore business resources available online. It claims to be the "largest and most comprehensive free resource of small business information" and it supports the claim with hundreds and hundreds of links to online resources organized into topics such as:

- Starting a Business
- Sales & Marketing
- Financial Management
- Personnel Management
- Buying & Selling a Business
- General Management
- International Trade
- Personal Skills, and
- Inspirational Stuff

Their Small Business Directory is worth a bookmark all by itself, offering links to the topics above as well as links to business magazines, newsgroups, government sites, discussion lists, sites with "free stuff," and the now ubiquitous link to Amazon.com for buying business books online.

Small Business Knowledge Base also offers its own CD-ROM, "Managing a Small Business," which expands upon the information offered online.

If you don't have time for anything else and have no interest at all in being an entrepreneur you still owe it to yourself to scan the Inspirational Stuff. Some of the anecdotes are well-worn chestnuts but all are worth the re-telling.

For example, a message from United Technologies Corporation published in the Wall Street Journal, pointed out:

- R.H. Macy failed seven times before his store in New York caught on.
- English novelist John Creasey got 753 rejection slips before he published 564 books.
- Babe Ruth struck out 1,330 times, but he also hit 714 home runs.

So. Is this the year you strike out on your own?

Entrepreneur Test (http://www.bizmove.com/other/quiz/htm)
Small Business Knowledge Base (http://www.bizmove.com)
Small Business Directory (http://www.bizmove.com/directory/index.htm)
Managing a Small Business (http://www.bizmove.com/other/cdpage.htm)
Inspirational Stuff (http://www.bizmove.com/inspiring.htm)

If you don't have time for anything else and have no interest at all in being an entrepreneur you still owe it to yourself to scan the Inspirational Stuff.

To Win in Business ... Know the SCORE

Many a brave entrepreneur has entered the fray armed with a brilliant idea, dauntless enthusiasm, indomitable self-confidence ... and the basic premise that it's "what you know rather than who you know" that determines business success.

And many a bloodied warrior has returned from the business battlefield having learned at high cost that there's an irony to that proverb: if "what you know" is that "it's who you know that counts" then what you know will indeed determine your success.

If you're thinking about starting a new business (or jump-starting a lagging one) don't despair if you're afraid you don't know the "who" that counts. There's help online.

... think of the SCORE volunteers as the grizzled veterans from the trenches who're responsible for keeping the rookies alive in their first fire fight. They've been there. Done that.

Since August of 1997 SCORE (Service Corps of Retired Executives) has used its Website to offer business advice to small businesses and entrepreneurs and the offerings rate three thumbs up!

For those who've never heard of it, SCORE is a resource partner with the government's Small Business Administration. It's staffed by volunteers. It offers general advice and specific counseling one-on-one. It costs nothing.

Forget the adage "worth what you pay for it."

This is one of those services that subverts the reputation of most government operations. It's good. It's helpful. It helping people help people.

SCORE has more than 12,000 volunteers in almost 400 chapters across the country. It was formed in 1964 and has served almost 4 million people. More than a quarter million people took part in workshops or counseling sessions in 1996 when over a million hours of time were donated by volunteers.

If you like military analogies for business (campaigns, strategies, tactics) think of the SCORE volunteers as the grizzled veterans from the trenches who're responsible for keeping the rookies alive in their first fire fight. They've been there. Done that.

In some cases SCORE volunteers are still actively running businesses. Most are retired. All receive special training before they're accepted as counselors — don't worry about having your ideas stolen or falling under the influence of the unscrupulous.

Using the ZIP Code form or geographic map locator you can find the SCORE office nearest you and call to set up a meeting with a counselor on specific problems you're having with your business.

Need specific help for your industry? Use Get Email Counseling: check the nearly 700 different categories of expertise that are listed and send your question by email. You may never get to meet your counselor if he or she is across the country but you will certainly get a response.

Wondering about what's available online? Visit Business Resources Index. It's a small but growing list of such links as a Loan Amortization Calculator, Chambers of Commerce, Franchising Opportunities, Patent laws and Trade Shows.

Business Hotlinks offers links to Associations, Commercial Services, Government Websites, Entrepreneurial Resources and online publications.

Can this work for you?

Check out the growing number of "Client Successes." These are real people who got help and agreed to have their stories told. You can contact them by phone, fax or email. People like April Lougheed in Indianapolis who sought counseling for her home-based Internet business which generated only $15,000 annually, or Danny O'Neill in Kansas City who started a coffee bean wholesale business in his basement and now has a multi-million dollar corporation.

SCORE also conducts more than 4,000 local workshops and seminars across the country on topics such as Obtaining Financing, Developing a Business Plan and Protecting Your Invention.

Is it what you know or who you know that counts? Go to SCORE. See for yourself.

SCORE (http://www.score.org)
Get Email Counseling (http://www.score.org/online/)
Business Resources Index (http://www.score.org/resourceindex/resource.html)
Business Hotlinks (http://www.score.org/businesslinks)
Client Sucessses (http://www.score.org/success)

Check out the growing number of "Client Successes." These are real people who got help and agreed to have their stories told.

Working Moms Find Internet Refuge

The plea posted on the Rant Board says it all for millions of working moms who are at the end of their tether:

"I CAN'T TAKE IT ANY MORE!!!!"

Instead of taking the next Greyhound out of town on a one-way ticket this young mom went online to share her frustrations with the growing sisterhood that is learning to share and nurture and support each other online.

"I have a 3 & 4 year old," wrote Cheryl, "a husband and a father, all of which do not help. I work full time at least 10 hrs a day, I live roughly 45 to 50 min one way from my office, my house is a mess, my yard is a mess (we live on 11 acres), my life is a mess. I can't seem to get the laundry done let alone shave my legs!!!! and now they want animals, who's gonna feed the @#$&* horse??? Oh, well gotta get back to work. Thanks for listening."

The site Cheryl turned to for help was the Working Mom's Internet Refuge, a growing collection of links and resources for moms who are facing the challenges of being everything to everyone.

Suddenly an "impromptu community" was created; an idea germinated; a new Website emerged.

The site was born of a real working mom's cry for help to members of a Web design listgroup. She was flooded with responses almost immediately. Suddenly an "impromptu community" was created; an idea germinated; a new Website emerged.

The Refuge's information is laid out clearly so you can zoom in on the immediate problem that's driving you nuts. For instance, the topics include information about:

Working Moms' Internet Refuge
you are not alone!

- Family: Pediatrics for Parents, Mothering, Single Moms, New Moms, family health notes and helpful tips on problems that need to be worked out such as having two kids share a room
- Career: Networking Moms, Women and Money, Survival Guide, Smart Questions, Small Business, Job Flexibility, Entrepreneurial Parent
- Personal: suggestions on topics like how to become a better mom than you had or what the latest breast cancer research is showing
- Art of Juggling: stories and tips from moms who've been there and juggled that including having a full house, a home office and kids in the office who aren't a distraction.
- Dad's Voice: words from the frontline for the two million stay-at-home dads who keep things together while Mom's at work
- What's for Dinner: recipes for great meals that can be whipped up in a jiffy
- Essential Indulgences: reducing stress, relaxing, aromatherapy, bath oils, massage — you know you deserve it
- Rant Board: a listserv where you may join the daily discussion, listen, talk or just lurk in the background

Was there help for Cheryl? You bet.

"Give up the long shifts, move closer to work, give up the acreage or give up your family, cause you can't have it all," wrote Gina. "Please reprioritize and give your family a happier, smiling mom they will cherish more than the house, the cars or the 11 acres!"

The Working Moms behind the title are Kim Foglia, a Website developer in Long Island, NY who uttered the first cry for help, Terry Klutymans, a Website developer in Vancouver, British Columbia, Liv Faret, an advertising professional in Santa Monica, CA, and Kris Kendrick, a creative director for a Website development company. Between them they have five children aged from one to 17 and they obviously speak from experience.

Working Mom's Internet Refuge (http://www.moms-refuge.com)

"Please reprioritize and give your family a happier, smiling mom they will cherish more than the house, the cars or the 11 acres!"

For Fabulous Fortunes, Focus on Forbes 400

Gold-diggers and gawkers at the rich and famous, here's your Website! Whether you simply admire those who are wildly successful, or you're digging for gold in the form of a rich spouse or a generous gift to your favorite charity, you'll want to browse this list.

Forbes Magazine's list of the 400 richest people in America can be found at the Forbes home page. Just type "Forbes 400" into the search engine at the site.

Since 1982, the annually updated list has offered a strange snapshot of the economy. Such prodigies as Microsoft's Bill Gates are there. He topped the list for the sixth time in 1999, adding $25 billion to his net worth — "roughly $3 million an hour" as they gently put it. Microsoft co-founder Paul Allen climbed to second place with a net worth of $40 billion, displacing legendary Warren Buffett of Berkshire Hathaway who was credited with "only" $31 billion.

Number four was another Microsoftie, company president Steven Ballmer, whose net worth topped $23 billion.

Forbes also has a Daily Wealth Index, available only online, so you can see how your favorite technology multi-billionaires' fortunes are holding up.

They're not all computer geeks. There's Amazon.com founder Jeff Bezos, television star Oprah Winfrey, movie mogul Steven Spielberg and families like the Wal-Mart Waltons, the Fords, the Rockefellers, and the Mellons.

The list comes out each October, based on net worth as of the first of September. In 1999 you had to have $625 million to be included. (When I last checked they ranked 243 American billionaires.)

Forbes also has a Daily Wealth Index, available only online, so you can see how your favorite technology multi-billionaires' fortunes are holding up.

A month after the magazine was published, Mr. Gates' net worth had decreased $14 billion; Allen's fortune had dropped to $26 billion; Ballmer's fell to $21 billion.

Buffett didn't even rate a ranking.

There are scads of sub-rankings, including Microsofties, Cable Guys, the Berkshire Bunch,

Financiers, Inheritors, Landlords and the Wives Club. Other listings count families, near misses and drop-outs.

If you want to connect only with the super rich in a certain state or area of endeavor, or even age and marital status, you can create a custom list from Forbes' database.

In addition to the searchable database, you can read articles from issues dating back to 1996.

Some are gossipy as you could wish and others are downright inspirational. Some contain practical how-to tips if you are set on joining the list one day.

I particularly enjoyed the one from the 1997 issue about photographing the rich, "Why can't billionaires grow up?" by Joe Queenan. He pokes fun at those who "opted for the silly look," in contrast to [1996's] "dignified" shot of Paul Mellon. Instead one posed with a guitar, another in a suit and sneakers and a third in workout gear.

"[O]ne gets the definite impression that they simply think that they are unbelievably cool," writes Queenan. Instead of being cool, though, he says "They look like middle-aged men whose kids — and employees — probably wish they'd get a clue."

In contrast, Mellon, who ranked 123rd in October 1998 and died February 2, 1999 at age 91, was as admired for his generosity as for his dignity. In his will, he left millions of dollars and priceless paintings to a number of cultural and educational institutions, including the National Gallery of Art in Washington which was founded by his father, Andrew. (His money? He got it the old-fashioned way: inheritance.)

Other articles include examinations of how these people got so rich, how much they give away and how they live and spend their money.

There's one on how to pass wealth on to your descendants and avoid the "shirtsleeves to shirtsleeves in three generations" fate of many family fortunes.

Forbes Magazine (http://www.forbes.com)
The Forbes 400 (http://www.forbes.com/forbes/Section/400.htm)
Daily Wealth Index (http://www.forbes.com/gates/daily.asp)
Queenan article (http://www.forbes.com/forbes/97/1013/6008046a.htm)

Instead of being cool, though, he says "They look like middle-aged men whose kids— and employees— probably wish they'd get a clue."

Armchair Millionaire Teaches Investment Strategies

To early screen-agers (first generation to be raised with televisions) the name John Beresford Tipton, announced in slow deliberate cadences by a man who introduced himself with the words "Hello, my name is Michael Anthony..." brings a thrill of expectation.

"I'm gonna be rich," they think. "I'm gonna be a millionaire!"

Back in the fifties, when a million dollars was a lot of money and the federal budget only extended into billions, "The Millionaire" was a television program that captured the popular imagination.

Tipton, an eccentric multi-millionaire who never appeared on screen, picked regular people at random and sent out his agent, Michael Anthony, to present cashier's checks for a million dollars tax free. The rest of the program was then devoted to seeing how sudden wealth would affect the recipients.

The concept was awe-inspiring; how could a single person possibly spend all that money?

Now, in the nineties, when the number of American millionaires is approaching a million, it is not unusual to read of million-dollar salaries for near-anonymous third-basemen. But for most of us it is still just a dream.

However, if being a millionaire is still one of your dreams you can take a quick reality check on your strategies at the Armchair Millionaire Website where free investment advice offers to help you build your retirement portfolio.

If you don't yet have a retirement plan maybe you'd better reconsider.

In one of many peppy asides that are sprinkled over the site, the AM points out that a recent survey of 18 to 34-year-old Americans shows "46% believed in the existence of extraterrestrials while only 28% believed Social Security would still be around when they retired."

In another, the question "How long does it take to become a millionaire?" leads to a simple guess list: Hypothetical Susan earns $45,000 per year and saves $18.50 a day, half of which goes into regular savings, half into an IRA, earning an average 10.5% annual return. How long before she's a millionaire?

... a recent survey of 18 to 34-year-old Americans shows "46% believed in the existence of extraterrestrials while only 28% believed Social Security would still be around when they retired."

If you guessed 26 years, you're right on the money. If you're in her same financial shoes yourself, well ... are you there yet?

The AM is supported by accounting software giant Intuit but you don't need their programs to enjoy the site. It was created by Lewis Schiff, 28, an early Web investment guru who launched Worth Online on AOL and created the original "Five Steps to Financial Freedom." Schiff's team includes a handful of Gen-Xers in New York and financial advisor John Bowen in California, the theorist behind their passive investing strategies.

The AM's plan is based on a basic strategy of investing in three broad market funds and using Five Steps to Financial Freedom which are described simply without jargon. There's also a Gallery of Investors where regular people describe their investing practices. A message board and chat room allow visitors to exchange ideas and seek advice.

A brief weekly collection of tips and insights is offered as Poor Rich's Almanac. The July issue of Mutual Funds magazine is quoted, for example, showing that $1 invested in 1871 in a diversified portfolio of US stocks would have grown to $33,770 today while a dollar invested in US Treasury bonds would be worth only $9.88.

Because everyone always likes to see how other people are doing the AM offers a look at the real-life Model Portfolio of investments for Schiff and his wife Lynette. You can track their investments on a weekly basis and read discussions of their strategies and tactics.

Unfortunately for the Schiffs, using the AM program, their portfolio declined 1.3% to $86,572 between mid-March and mid-June of 1998. A year later, however it was up to $104,604.35.

As you might expect, Poor Rich's Almanac in mid-June included the warning "... don't forget that investing in the stock market is a long-term endeavor, and that short-term declines are natural and to be expected."

Armchair Millionaire (http://www.armchairmillionaire.com)
Five Steps to Financial Freedom (http://www.armchairmillionaire.com/fivesteps/)
Gallery of Investors (http://www.armchairmillionaire.com/gallery/)
Poor Rich's Almanac (http://www.armchairmillionaire.com/poorrich/)
Model Portfolio (http://www.armchairmillionaire.com/portfolio/)

... $1 invested in 1871 in a diversified portfolio of US stocks would have grown to $33,770 today while a dollar invested in US Treasury bonds would be worth only $9.88.

Online Buying Is Easier, Faster — More Competitive

"When I get a little money, I buy books. If there is any left over, I buy food."

One of those omnipresent financial experts I'm always stumbling over in magazines has suggested we freeze our credit card spending. Literally.

He suggested putting credit cards in plastic cups of water in the freezer. When the urge to charge hits, you have to wait until the ice has melted before you can use your card. No fair using the microwave to speed things up — after all just imagine what those invisible rays might do the magnetic strip on the back.

Anyway, the idea is that by the time you can fish your card out, you'll be able to tell whether your purchase is practical or impulsive.

Buying stuff on the Internet is probably safer if you follow the expert's advice, particularly if you can't read the number through the ice. In other words, there are lots of good bargains out there, but it pays to do your homework before committing to a purchase.

Online, buying things gets easier and faster every day. Examples include 1-Click ordering at Amazon.com and the auction house frenzy at Onsale.com. There are myriad opportunities to buy something you've always wanted — or something you'll never look at again...

Recently I was visiting a cyber-savvy uncle in California. He's 80-something, though you wouldn't know it to look at him. One morning he got an email from a nephew-by-marriage in Albany, NY., with a book recommendation. Within seconds, literally, my uncle had logged onto Amazon and ordered Great Books by David Denby. It arrived the day I left. He was very pleased.

Amazon.com keeps your credit card info in their database, securely of course. Enter it once and you can buy on impulse from then on, even when the credit card is safely stowed between the ice cream and the frozen fish.

This may be fine, if you are disciplined enough, or truly passionate about books.

I thought of Erasmus's oft-quoted line: "When I get a little money, I buy books. If there is any left over, I buy food."

Onsale Online Auction Supersite adds competition to online shopping. The auctions are live, virtually.

Here you can bid on computers, consumer electronics, sports equipment and all the other must-have accessories of the modern world.

They start at ridiculously low prices, too. If you are lucky you might come away with a real steal. Or you might find the same item for sale at a better price from the computer store down the road. Or you might buy last year's model at this year's price.

Buyer beware. Make sure you know what you are getting.

When I visited one day, a lot of 131 U.S. Robotics PalmPilot #5000 organizers were about to go on sale at an opening bid of $99. I've never owned one. It sounded like a good deal.

When I called my local computer retailer, I discovered it was an older version of the popular device. The current model, the PalmPilot Professional model sells there for $299. The older model at a third the price might be just what you need, but be sure.

At the same time, bids were heating up on a HyperData notebook computer with lots of speed and memory. Bids began at $199. By the time I visited they were up to $1,629.

How good a deal is that? Are those bidders getting carried away, or not? I looked up HyperData computers at CNet's Computers.com site, and couldn't find any information or reviews. Nor could I find the exact same computer or any prices at the HyperData Direct Website, but there was a phone number.

If I were tempted to bid on this one, I'd call the HyperData Sales Hotline first to find the list prices and model year.

According to the counter at the site, more than four million bids have been placed in the various ongoing auctions. I looked longingly at several things, such as a factory refurbished, water resistant portable CD player with car adapter starting at $9, and a Xerox Document HomeCentre color printer, copier and scanner starting at $1 (it was up $181 when I visited, with more than 24 hours to go).

But I resisted. For now. I think I might go buy a book instead.

Amazon.com (http://www.amazon.com)
Great books (http://www.amazon.com/exec/obidos/ISBN=0684835339/4805-9632618-739203)
Onsale (http://www.onsale.com/)
Computers.com (http://www.computers.com)
HyperData (http://www.hyperdatadirect.com/)

If you are lucky you might come away with a real steal. Or you might find the same item for sale at a better price from the computer store down the road. Or you might buy last year's model at this year's price...

Do You Know Where Your 401(k) Is?

If you have a 401(k) at work, may I ask how much attention are you paying to it? Do you really understand how the whole thing works?

401 Kafé

I'm not trying to be nosy. If you're like most of us you'd probably rather have a root canal than worry about second-guessing your 401(k) plan administrator. But then again, it is your money isn't it?

If you're interested enough in your future financial well-being to allow the deductions from your paycheck you may want to drop into 401 Kafé online. You'll be surprised by some of the habitués.

It has an awkward looking name, but this "community resource for 401(k) participants" has answers to serious questions, tips, quizzes, articles and boards where investors in employer-sponsored retirement plans can share information and concerns.

It's a site provided for its members by San Francisco-based 401(k) Forum, an online investment advisor, but there is much here for visitors. If you're an investment newbie, or if you just haven't been paying much attention up until now, you can start with the ABC's of 401(k) Plans.

As you'd expect, this part begins with the basics: "401(k) plans are retirement vehicles that allow employees to save for their own retirement. This type of plan was named for section 401(k) of the Internal Revenue Code, which permits employees of qualifying companies to set aside tax-deferred funds."

One of the contributors to this site, and a board member of 401(k) Forum, is Ted Benna, the former benefits consultant who figured out the 401(k) plan in the first place. Talk about going to the source: this guy wrote the book.

According to his bio at the site, Benna attributes his idea to "divine inspiration."

Talk about going to the source: this guy wrote the book.

He "was actually thinking of quitting benefits consulting altogether. He was dissatisfied because companies wanted him to design retirement plans that were more advantageous to top professionals than to their lower-paid employees.

"I had been thinking of getting out of consulting and working for a ministry of some type, and that's where the prayer came in. It was during this period that the 401(k) hit out of the blue."

He pored over the tax code and noticed that the pre-tax saving and employer matching contributions that are the core of the plan were not forbidden by its section 401(k). It may not sound like much, but it was the opening he needed. The IRS approved it in 1981 and issued official regulations ten years later.

Benna writes a regular column for 401Kafé called Ted's Table, where he answers questions sent in by readers. Other columns include Money Manager where 401(k) Forum analysts take on investment issues, and What's Brewing with news about developments and issues.

A recent What's Brewing article, Fee Fairy Tale, takes on the issue of fees: how to calculate them, what they buy, and what questions to ask your benefits department about them. There are links to Department of Labor publications, as well as other Internet resources. Though it's written in fractured fairy tale style, the underlying facts are straightforward. It's cute but not dumb.

The 401Kafé FAQ has questions from the simplest "What is a 401(k)?" to more complicated ones concerning taxes, rollovers, employer contributions and whether it's a good idea to take out a loan on your 401(k).

One FAQ section deals with commonly used terms such as risk, diversification, and the definition of different types of funds. There is also a large glossary at the site.

If you're pretty sure you're well-informed about all that, you can take a quiz or two to confirm it.

If you aren't so sure, 401Kafé can help you brush up on what you need to know. Wall Street 101 starts with Investment Basics, then goes on to sections titled Risk, Diversify, Asset Allocation and Your Place in the Market. Each section ends up with a brief quiz.

Whatever size your company, whatever plan administrator it uses to manage your 401(k), you will find information here to help you understand and, if necessary, suggest improvements in the way it's done. After all, it's your money, right?

401Kafé (http://www.401kafe.com/)
ABC's of 401(k) plans (http://www.401kafe.com/education/abc_intro.html)
Ted's Bio (http://www.401kafe.com/tips/teds_bio.html)
Ted's Table (http://www.401kafe.com/tips/teds_table.html)
FAQ (http://www.401kafe.com/faq/index.html)
What's Brewing (http://www.401kafe.com/tips/brewing.html)

Though it's written in fractured fairy tale style, the underlying facts are straightforward. It's cute but not dumb.

Online Counselors Offer Bankruptcy Alternatives

What do you do when the money runs out, the credit cards go flat, the bills pile up and the collection agencies start wearing out your telephone?

Want to bail out? Get a fresh start? File for bankruptcy?

For millions of Americans, declaring bankruptcy may be the only way to cope with a crushing burden of debt. More than 1.4 million filed for personal bankruptcy in 1997 — an almost 50% increase over 1992 at the height of the last recession.

That number is on the increase again with second quarter filings setting a record for the highest number of bankruptcies ever, according to the American Bankruptcy Institute.

Despite the record increase in bankruptcies, a growing number of equally financially-pressed consumers are turning to online counseling services to find ways to climb out of debt. They're laying out their resources, exposing their liabilities and working out debt management plans that can launch them on a course of future fiscal stability.

The counseling is free — paid for by the creditors themselves who would rather have small payments over time than no payments at all from bankrupt debtors.

The counseling is free — paid for by the creditors themselves who would rather have small payments over time than no payments at all from bankrupt debtors.

Consumer Credit Counseling Service of Houston, TX offers its services to people anywhere on the globe. Counseling is confidential and can be conducted by email, fax, telephone or old-fashioned snail mail.

Their Website offers a variety of easy-to-understand consumer resources including "Dear Susan & Co." a friendly Q&A reference on two dozen topics ranging from Bankruptcy to Working with Creditors.

Written by Susan Quick, director of Money Management International in Farmville, VA, the growing advice column answers real questions from regular folks who are facing trying times financially.

If misery loves company, people in financial stress will find real comfort in reading about the painful situations other consumers get themselves into.

For example:

- Bankruptcy: Lisa asks whether she'll be able to buy a home if she files for bankruptcy; bankruptcy stays on your record for 10 years and makes it very difficult to buy a home or rent an apartment, answers Susan; any major purchase will likely require a much higher down payment and higher than normal interest rates.
- College Debt: Tim says he hasn't made any effort to pay back $13,000 in student loans and now he's being threatened with a 45% penalty; can they do that? Yes, says Susan, the government can garnish your wages, add penalties and possibly even jail time. Ouch.
- Credit Cards: John from Indiana writes to ask if it's legal for his credit card company to raise his interest rate from 7.9% to 12.9% to 19.9% to 25.9%. You bet, says Susan, it's in the fine print on the original agreement you signed; the only recourse is to quit charging and pay it off.

In almost every case, of course, writers are encouraged to call their local Consumer Credit Counseling Service or the toll-free telephone line at Money Management International.

If you enter into a debt management plan with MMI your creditors are asked to accept a payment plan arranged by your MMI counselor to fit your current circumstances. You begin to make monthly payments to a creditor's trust account maintained by MMI and they in turn pay your creditors.

MMI recently introduced MoneyWise, a quarterly newsletter online. The premiere issue offers very basic tips on money management with articles on home equity borrowing, grocery shopping, auto repair, saving energy and involving teenagers in money decisions.

It's not rocket science but it's a good place to start if you're thinking seriously about getting control of your finances for the first time.

American Bankruptcy Institute (http://www.abiworld.org/media/newmediafront.html)
Consumer Credit Counseling Service (http://www.powersource.com/cccs/default.html)
Money Management International (http://www.mmintl.org/)
MoneyWise (http://www.mmintl.org/news/default.html)

It's not rocket science but it's a good place to start if you're thinking seriously about getting control of your finances for the first time.

Speculators Inflate "Dot-Coms"

The Economist

Frenzy, bubble and binge are words reporters and pundits use freely these days to describe the wild gyrations in the value of Internet-related stocks. Investors' interest in companies whose names end in "dot-com" — no matter what those companies actually DO — seems virtually undiscriminating.

Alan Greenspan, chairman of the Federal Reserve Bank, weighed into the debate early, telling the US Senate Budget Committee that there was "something fundamentally potentially sound under" the hype surrounding Internet stocks. But, before you get too exuberant, Greenspan also noted that most small companies whose stock prices have skyrocketed are "almost sure to fail."

Greenspan isn't the only one who is taking a guarded attitude toward this extraordinary market. At the end of January 1999, the Economist Magazine ran online editorials with discouraging titles like "When the bubble bursts" and "Why Internet shares will fall."

Day traders, the Economist editorial writer points out, are partly responsible for the "Internet phenomenon."

"Many spend seven or eight hours a day online, and for them the Internet companies they invest in take on an unreal stature. As the virtual world displaces the physical, the idea that Yahoo! could be bigger and more important than Boeing or Eastman Kodak somehow becomes plausible. For most day traders, conventional market valuations derived from future profits are for idiots who just don't get it."

When the frenzy dies down and the bubble bursts and the dust clears, what will remain standing?

While day traders and financial gurus rile up the stock markets and fret about the eventual fallout, I find myself wondering about the companies themselves.

When the frenzy dies down and the bubble bursts and the dust clears, what will remain standing? According to the Economist, "Even after an Internet crash, there would be enough wealth to back good ideas."

In the meantime, it's kind of fun to look at the home pages of these high flyers and try to figure out whether they're a sound and light show operated by a little man behind a curtain, like the Wonderful Wizard of Oz, or on their way to places beside the rail and steel companies of late 19th Century in the Pantheon of capitalistic success.

I've used three of those frequently mentioned and have come to rely on them.

Yahoo!, the Internet's first search engine, is an easy-to-use way to get all kinds of information quickly. What makes Yahoo! different from other search engines is that real live employees look at all the Websites it catalogues. Their database isn't made up of sites picked out by autobots or algorithms. It doesn't try to dazzle you with graphics, but it lets you find what you want within a controlled range of Internet sites. It is constantly improving, but allows you to explore and take advantage of the change and new offerings at your leisure.

Amazon.com, the world's largest bookstore, has saved my bacon more than once, when I've waited too long to buy a birthday or other present. Like Yahoo!, you can get as much or as little from it as you wish. From book clubs and recommendations to news of awards and interviews with authors, it's a booklover's playground. You can also buy music, videos, software, hardware — with the introduction of "z-Shops" in 1999 there's probably anything you can imagine.

Although they have yet to make a profit, Amazon.com is building market-share hand over fist. Their willingness to suffer massive losses while they follow a business strategy of "under-promising and over-delivering" daunts even the most formidable competitors.

AOL — what can you say about a company with 20 million subscribers relying on it for access to the Internet? Expert Netsurfers scoff at AOL, and refer to it as "training wheels" for the Internet user. Others have compared it to a police state where chat rooms are vigorously patrolled by AOL employees who have the power to expel the abusive or profane.

All those AOL subscribers don't much care. It's convenient, comprehensive, and a great way to stay in touch with friends and relatives all over the world. Once you get used to the Internet, you may want to branch out. In the meantime, what's wrong with training wheels?

Are they the blue chip companies of the future? Maybe. They've sure made the Internet a more useful, accessible place.

There is undoubtedly something of value underlying all these stocks but, like the conclusion of the speculative frenzy that erupted in 17th Century Holland on the introduction of tulips from Turkey, when the supply of "dot-coms" finally sates market demand there will be an inevitable correction. When? Ah, now that's a question worthy of speculation.

The Economist (http://www.economist.com)
Yahoo! (http://www.yahoo.com)
Tulip bulb speculation (http://www.derivatives.com/comix/1996/9602/9602cx1.html)

... when the supply of "dot-coms" finally sates market demand there will be an inevitable correction.

Office.com Offers Business Basics

Another "comprehensive site for business"? What are they trying to sell us this time? you well might ask.

The answer is phone service, but don't let that put you off.

Serious business people don't have time to read every book and online article that's been written about doing business. That's understood. You're too busy running your business to spend a whole lot of time reading about how to do it.

If you want to do a little Web surfing, though, you could do worse than checking out Office.com. Although it's provided by WinStar Communications, Inc., a company that sells telecommunication and broadband services, the sales pitch is muted. If you want to know more about the company, you must click a link and go to WinStar's own site.

At Office.com, you'll find straightforward, no nonsense articles about business basics.

Under the heading "Business Tools" they promise "step-by-step training covering the key aspects of operating a thriving business." So, who needs an MBA, anyway?

There are articles about preparing a balance sheet, analyzing profitability, valuing your business and preparing your company to go public. Other articles include tips on conducting a market analysis, analyzing your competition, and creating a direct mail package.

A series of articles on Personalization Strategies to Attract and Retain Customers discusses the various technologies available for different types of businesses, personalizing your Web-based business, and thoughts about what works and what doesn't. There are links to various Websites that illustrate points made in the articles.

...straightforward, no nonsense articles about business basics.

Under "Smart Business" there are weekly articles and an archive. Topics such as Creating a Corporate Culture, Bridging Generation Gaps at the Office, and Recruiting in a Global Employee Market are certainly worth considering.

There are profiles of successful entrepreneurs such as Ray Sozzi, founder, president and CEO of Student Advantage, a membership purchasing program for college students. Sozzi had the idea of using the purchasing power of the millions of US college students to secure discounts on purchase when he was a student himself. Now age 30, he has about 200 employees, runs the the country's largest discount network for college students and was named Ernst & Young's Entrepreneur of the Year in 1998.

Other profiled entrepreneurs provide a fascinating glimpse into what people are doing and what is proving successful. Yomega Corp is making a splash with high performance yo-yos, for example and an article analyses its success and traces its history. If you haven't bought a yo-yo in the past two decades or so, you'll be amazed at what's happening. Then there's iPrint, an interactive, online commercial print shop where customers can design and order everything from printed stationery to coffee mugs. And there are others.

These profiles alone make a visit to Office.com valuable.

There's also advice about legal issues faced by small businesses, including contracts, intellectual property protection and so on. Human resources topics include articles about hiring, time management, and nurturing "intrapreneurial" employees. I hadn't heard that word before, but discovered here that "'Intrapreneur' is the name given to such innovative employees who come up with their own ideas and then bring those ideas to life with the assistance and resources offered by their employers." Definitely worth nurturing, I'd say.

The site is easy to navigate and well designed. If you like it, you can subscribe to a newsletter that will keep you up to date on developments at the site.

So do you need an MBA? I have no idea, but if you've started a business and want it to thrive, or if your business is thriving and you don't know what to do next, you might find the answers to your questions here.

Office.com (http://www.office.com)
WinStar Communications, Inc. (http://www.winstar.com)
Student Advantage (http://www.studentadvantage.com/)
Yomega Corp (http://www.yomega.com/)
IPrint (http://www.iprint.com)

Other profiled entrepreneurs provide a fascinating glimpse into what people are doing and what is proving successful.

Business Schools Focus on Morality and Ethics

When most of the national media and much of Washington was seemingly mesmerized by speculation on the President's indiscretions it seemed in early 1999 that the topic of morality and ethics had become much like the weather.

It is not so much that it is "changeable" but, as Will Rogers said, "Everybody talks about the weather but no one does anything about it."

What are people to think about morality in their private lives when the practice of morality in public life seems to leave so much to be, er, ... desired?

It is a matter of intense interest in the business world because it not only affects behavior and morale in the short term, it affects the bottom line in the long term.

Major North American graduate business schools all offer courses in ethics and many of them have begun to publish extensive materials on the Internet including Dartmouth's Institute for the Study of Applied and Professional Ethics, the University of British Columbia's Centre for Applied Ethics, University of Pennsylvania's Wharton Business School Zicklin Center, and the University of Virginia's Olsson Center.

What are people to think about morality in their private lives when the practice of morality in public life seems to leave so much to be, er, ... desired?

Wharton publishes an electronic newsletter which covers such topics as "Outlawing Transnational Bribery Through the World Trade Organization" and the Japanese approach to business ethics called "moralogy."

In addition to descriptions of course offerings and research projects they also offer case studies of both real and fictitious companies. Consider, for instance, the issue of "false statements" in business transactions.

How do you feel about:

• a negotiator for a local teachers' union who knows the union cannot afford a strike and has the authority to settle for a 5% raise; he thinks he can get 8% and additional prep time but tells the school negotiator he must get 10% or a strike will be impossible to avoid.

• a 52-year old engineer applying for a job learns that the company never hires anyone over 50 so he changes his resume to show his age as 45 and uses Grecian formula to color his gray hairs before the interview.

- the proper response for an employee who was caught embezzling but allowed to resign rather than be fired and prosecuted; he applies for a job with another firm that checks his references and asks you whether he has ever been "convicted" of any crime.

Every issue that seems black and white in theory begins to blur at the edges in the real world. The good news is that future leaders of business are beginning to focus on the issue at an earlier stage.

In England, National Westminster Bank and The Times newspaper used to sponsor an annual Business Ethics competition each spring for UK college undergraduates. The winner received £3000 (US $4,500). Another £3000 was awarded to the winner's college. There were smaller awards for second and third place winners.

The competition reflected "the appreciation among a growing number of companies that many short term solutions to business problems may have harmful long term consequences for their relationships with key stakeholders, and therefore with profits."

Contestants had to submit a 1,000-word essay to solve a fictitious business dilemma. In 1999 the challenge was to decide between two courses of action after a military coup in a developing country in which your company has been profitably conducting business for many years. The new government was "characterised by an unwillingness to respect human rights."

Should you (a) withdraw your company from the country or (b) work to change the government to that of a democratic nature?

There's no "right" answer. As the entry rules explained "The judges are looking for evidence of reasoning and moral judgement, rather than technical knowledge, and having a fresh pair of eyes could help you to see the wood from the trees."

Shortly after NatWest dropped its sponsorship of the contest the military seized control of the government of Pakistan. Pity. Would have been interesting to see the results.

Inst. for the Study of Applied and Professional Ethics (http://www.dartmouth.edu/artsci/ethicsinst/)
University of British Columbia's Centre for Applied Ethics (http://www.ethics.ubc.ca/)
Wharton Business School Zicklin Center (http://rider.wharton.upenn.edu/~ethics/zicklin/research.html)
University of Virginia's Olsson Center (http://www.darden.virginia.edu/research/olsson/olsson.htm)
Wharton's Newsletter (http://rider.wharton.upenn.edu/~ethics/newsletter/fall97news1.pdf)
Case Studies: False Statements (http://rider.wharton.upenn.edu/~ethics/cases/false.htm)

Every issue that seems black and white in theory begins to blur at the edges in the real world.

Working Stiff Examines Changing Workplace

What is it with this economy?

Jobs, for instance. One day you hear about record layoffs, the next day, the news is that unemployment has never been lower. Workers don't know whether to be smug or scared.

And there's the matter of time. The ideal of fewer workers working more efficiently to produce more goods or services may actually have been carved out of the schedule of a Victorian workhouse with longer workdays and less personal time. What are beepers and telecommuting but electronic shackles as new math morphs 9-2-5 into 24-7?

If you've been wondering if this is any way to live you should visit "Working Stiff," a project of Web Lab, which takes on "the trials and tribulations of working life."

The staff — Editor and Co-Producer Jennifer Vogel, Co-Producer Robin Marks, and Art Director Adam Chapman — between them held many "McJobs" working in truck stops, hospital cafeterias, Orange Julius stands, and so on before embarking on journalism and design careers. They know what they are talking about.

This site may seem slightly Bolshie ... but it offers an honest forum for the real concerns of today's worker.

This site may seem slightly Bolshie to management types and older executives, but it offers an honest forum for the real concerns of today's worker.

Feature articles take on topics such as workplace safety, and how workers can protect themselves from abuses such as unpaid overtime and discrimination. Twisted Knickers is a guide to office romance. The Walls Have Eyes suggests ways to protect your privacy from bosses who can legally read your emails and monitor your phone conversations. Time Bandits takes a look at how our jobs are stealing personal time.

If Things are so Great, Why are You Broke? asks the question so many of us struggle with all the time. Author Doug Henwood, editor of Left Business Observer, contends that low inflation and unemployment masks the fact that "we're all slaving away at longer and longer business hours while incomes for poor and middle-income households are roughly the same as they were in 1973." He also notes that of the 30 job titles projected by the Bureau of Labor Statistics to show the largest job growth in the next ten years, almost two thirds will not require a college degree. Cashiers are at the top of the list.

Workplace Diaries, another section of the site, lets an office assistant, a high-tech worker, a bartender, a customer service representative, and a casino worker tell their own stories.

All those who ever worked at a job they hated because they were afraid to be broke will hear their thoughts (and fears) echoed in the workplace diary of a Silicon Valley tech writer. The young woman writes of being fired for not being enthusiastic enough about her work — which involved writing user manuals for software she wasn't able to use.

Shades of Dilbert!

There's also an advice column, a discussion board, and a Stress-O-Meter to help you determine how stressed you really are (as if you didn't know!)

An Action Guide has links to a wide variety of Websites, including government agencies, legal and activist resources, union and labor related groups, workplace gripe sites and some entertaining sites at the end to keep your blood pressure down (if you're a worker, not a boss...).

Web Lab is a program of the New York Foundation for the Arts, and is supported by grants from the Ford Foundation, PBS and various family foundations. It was founded to develop and support projects like Working Stiff, that "bring fresh perspective and new voices to the discussion of public issues."

Other projects include Reality Check, "an experimental dialogue on public issues to counter the effect of media saturation;" "Adoption: a gathering; Living with Suicide; POV Salon, "an experimental forum to support online dialogues and connections;" and WDF2, Web Development Fund Round Two.

Working Stiff (http://www.pbs.org/weblab/workingstiff/)
Web Lab (http://www.weblab.org)
Bureau of Labor Statistics (http://stats.bls.gov/blshome.html)
Occupations with largest job growth(http://stats.bls.gov/news.release/ecopro.table7.htm)

All those who ever worked at a job they hated because they were afraid to be broke will hear their thoughts (and fears) echoed...

Compensation Gap Continues to Widen

When you read a story about a high-flying corporate CEO like Disney's Michael Eisner getting an average pay package of over $126 million for each of the past five years do you smile, frown or keep a poker face and go about your own business?

In an era of ordinary news stories about extraordinary pay packages and instant dot-com millionaires it's sometimes hard to put figures like this into meaningful context.

Forbes Magazine tries to give perspective in its survey of executive compensation. The magazine points out that the top ten highest paid executives earned a combined total of $2.3 billion between 1994 and 1998 and held $6.4 billion worth of their stock.

Were they worth it?

The magazine notes that the companies that employ these gold-plated CEO's also had a five-year annual average total return of 40%. In the case of Gateway 2000 (which paid CEO and founder Theodore Waitt $147 million over the past five years), "shareholders have little reason to gripe: their stock has increased an average 48% per year since 1994."

That sort of comparison makes the huge salaries sound pretty reasonable but one group that doesn't think so is the AFL-CIO. With membership down to 14% of the labor force (from almost 40% four decades ago) the old union warhorse is updating its efforts and its image using some of the tools of the information revolution.

Their Executive PayWatch Website asks some serious questions about comparative compensation and sheds an entirely different light on the equation.

Consider their facts, collected under the heading of Runaway CEO Pay:

- average CEO compensation in 1980 was 44 times that of average factory workers; in 1990 it was 85 times; in 1998 it was 419 times greater
- if the current trend continues executive compensation will be 150,000 times the average worker compensation by the year 2050
- while factory wages increased 70% over the past 15 years, inflation rose 85%, corporate profits went up 145% and CEO compensation jumped 500%

... if the current trend continues executive compensation will be 150,000 times the average worker compensation by the year 2050

- if worker pay had increased at the same rate, factory workers would average $90,000 a year; the minimum wage would be almost $20/hour
- in 1996 factory wages increased 3%; inflation 3.3%, company profits 11% but CEO pay 54%

To its great credit, Executive PayWatch provides a CEO Compensation Index by Company that lets you check the S&P 500 corporations for yourself. (The data is taken from each company's own proxy statement filed with the Securities and Exchange Commission.)

For instance, search under Walt Disney and you'll discover that Michael Eisner earned "only" $5,768,243 in 1998 and has $102 million in unexercised stock options.

Click on the comparison button and you'll be asked to enter your own compensation, including salary, bonus, stock options, free country club memberships, luxury car or chauffeur service, no-interest loans, use of company resort home or penthouse suite and free financial planning services.

If you enter a modest $30,000 salary you get a calculated response: "You would have to work 192 years to equal Michael D. Eisner's 1998 compensation. You'd better get working, because you can't take a vacation until 2191 A.D."

If you click on their comparison of other workers' compensation, you discover Eisner's paycheck would have paid the salaries of "five Nobel prize winners, 17 average university presidents, 28 US presidents, 29 AFL-CIO presidents, 53 Chairmen of the Joint Chiefs of Staff, 226 average workers or 538 minimum-wage earners."

Check for yourself. Pick a company and look at the stats. If the figures seem so astronomical as to be unbelievable you might check with Forbes which also offers a regularly updated searchable database of Corporate America's Most Powerful People. [see page 52]

Survey of Executive Compensation (http://www.forbes.com/forbes/99/0517/6310202a.htm)
Executive PayWatch (http://aflcio.org/paywatch/)
Runaway CEO Pay (http://aflcio.org/paywatch/ceopay.htm)
Executive PayWatch Database (http://aflcio.org/cgi-bin/aflcio.pl)
Corporate America's Most Powerful People (http://www.forbes.com/tool/toolbox/ceo/)

"You would have to work 192 years to equal Michael D. Eisner's 1998 compensation."

Web Displays Spirituality of Business

The world of business is fast-paced, bottom line-oriented and, like Tennyson's nature, "red in tooth and claw." It's a world ruled by the principal of survival of the fittest.

Perhaps. But not always. There are plenty of examples of pragmatic businesspeople who look beyond the breathless competition of the marketplace to what they perceive as higher truths.

From wholehearted participation in good works — such as Habitat for Humanity, programs to feed and shelter the less fortunate, and prison ministries — to prayer breakfasts and people-centered corporate mission statements, the natural human tendency to spirituality persists, even in the business world.

I have heard top level executives discuss the importance of caring for their employees and creating a corporate culture that encourages employees to care about one another. Others meet regularly to pray and discuss scripture under the auspices of groups like Needle's Eye Ministries in Richmond, VA.

Some of these people are members of a specific religious group, others are seeking spirituality wherever it is to be found: in books, retreats, community and service.

Monasteries like The Abbey of New Clairvaux, in California, and The Abbey of Gethsemani in Kentucky, offer a place for business people and all others to make retreats. Just use your favorite search engine with the key word Benedictine or Trappist to find many more.

One of the most interesting sites devoted to spirituality in the business and professional world is the work of a former Wall Street Tycoon.

Sir John Templeton, a Tennessee native and Rhodes Scholar who started work in the middle of the Depression, soon opened a fund management group of his own and became a pioneer in the field of mutual funds. He was knighted by Britain's Queen Elizabeth in 1987.

PBS's Wall Street guru, Louis Rukeyser, calls him "the premier international investor of the 20th Century."

The Templeton group of mutual funds were sold to the Franklin Company in 1992 and became Franklin-Templeton.

Sir John went on to concentrate on spirituality. Of course it was not a new thing. His online bio notes, among other things, that Templeton "is known, for example, for beginning mutual

... the natural human tendency to spirituality persists, even in the business world.

funds' annual meetings with a prayer."

The John Templeton Foundation funds programs and publishes a variety of books on topics relating to science and religion, psychology, spirituality, current affairs, inspiration, and character development.

The Website contains information on the Templeton Prize for Progress in Religion which has been given every year since 1973 "to a living individual who has shown extraordinary originality advancing the world's understanding of God and/or spirituality."

The first recipient was Mother Theresa of Calcutta.

According to the description of the prize at the site, "Buddhism, Christianity, Hinduism, Islam and Jewish faiths have all been represented by prize recipients. Some, such as 1995's winner, mathematical physicist Paul Davies, adhere to no particular faith at all."

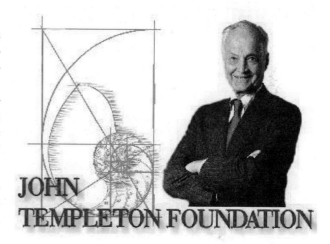

There is also a regularly changing excerpt from Templeton's book Worldwide Laws of Life, information on conferences and symposia, grant opportunities, and essays on a related topics.

It's an interesting site and an example of how one successful man has used his money and influence to "encourage a fresh appreciation of the critical importance of the moral and spiritual dimensions of life."

Habitat for Humanity (http://www.habitat.org/)
Needle's Eye Ministries (http://www.zip2.com/styleweekly/needleseye)
The Abbey of New Clairvaux (http://www.maxinet.com/trappist/)
Abbey of Gethsemani (http://www.monks.org/)
John Templeton Foundation (http://www.templeton.org/)
Franklin-Templeton (http://www.franklin-templeton.com/)
The Templeton Prize (http://templeton.org/prize/default.asp)

Templeton "is known, for example, for beginning mutual funds' annual meetings with a prayer."

Creativity Gone? Stretch Your Thinking Online

Businesses — at least some of them — spend real money on seminars and training sessions to help their workers solve problems and build creativity. Whether you agree that that's money well spent, or suspect the whole thing is bogus, you might profit from a visit to Hot Rod Your Head, a Website packed with intelligence builders, brain exercisers and intriguing stuff.

Like most self-help and self-improvement sites on the Internet, this one purports to explore the mind, body and soul. More about that later.

Whether you're stuck for the solution to a problem, want to increase your brain power, or just want an alternative to computer solitaire, you'll find something to encourage or entertain you here.

Business people who are seeking material for a do-it-yourself creativity-boosting seminar could do worse than a foraging trip through this site for suggestions. In fact, the forager might come away a true believer and actually hire a professional to run the event. You just never know.

... a Website packed with intelligence builders, brain exercisers and intriguing stuff.

On the other hand, there is a lot about this site that made me think that it was aimed at the 14-year-old boy in every grown man.

Sorry to sound sexist here, but what else am I supposed to make of the banner ads on various pages offering a sex quiz to determine how hot a lover you might be or touting the "world's best pickup lines"? They're like the ads in the back of comic books of my youth selling x-ray glasses that promised you could see through a girl's dress. There are naughty words here, though, so if you're offended by such, take my word for it that it's not worth a visit.

Most of the rest of the site is fun and helpful. It calls itself a "a Webzine that explores the limits of human potential," and when it's good, it's very good.

There are product reviews (some self-serving), problem-solving techniques, columns and discussions. There are exercises to build brain power, mind games and a whole page of links to IQ tests and such, including a European version, a MENSA Workout, brain tricks and quizzes as well as emotional, political, New Age and Jewelry IQ tests.

If you're serious about improving yourself, send your mind to Boot Camp. Even if you're neither young nor military-minded you'll get a good workout for your brains here. From word association games, math problems, and tangrams to a whole day of trying to see how quiet you can be, the brain workouts are thought-provoking as well as potentially self-improving.

Competitive types can take an IQ test before and after completing the boot camp to see if it actually does any good.

There are also puzzles and games for those of us who enjoy flexing our brains for fun. Games include Connect 4 and Othello as well as European and United States geography tests and others. Do you know where Moldova is? Or Latvia? See if your knowledge of geography is as good outside your particular area as it is within it. Africa and Asia are notably missing, but I hope they will be added soon.

I already told you about the "body" part of this site. Basically, you can skip it. There are plenty of better diet, fitness, and relationship sites all over the Internet. The "soul" section is a bit more fun, although some of the links were not working when I visited.

If you're intrigued by comparative religion, check out the deceptively simple "Dharma the Cat" comic strip link on the Soul page. Each installment of the adventures of a young Buddhist monk, Bodhi, his cat, Dharma, and mouse, Siam, is accompanied by commentary from practitioners of various religions, including Buddhism, Hinduism, Christianity, Judaism, Baha'i and Islam. It's an unusual approach.

There's a part on self-hypnosis, links to information on parapsychology and extrasensory perception, black magic, and a whole lot more.

Hot Rod Your Head (http://www.botree.com/)
IQ Tests (http://www.botree.com/iq.htm)
Brain Boot Camp (http://www.botree.com/boot/index.htm)
Dharma the Cat (http://www.dharmathecat.com/)

If you're serious about improving yourself, send your mind to Boot Camp ... you'll get a good workout for your brains here.

Net Thinkers Tell Businesses: Get a Clue

"The cluetrain stopped there four times a day for ten years and they never took delivery,"

Martin Luther would have been proud. However, the latest tribute to the great mediaeval German theologian is not an invitation to debate religious practices and principles but certainly a point of view that should shake conventional thinking.

The newest protest is the "Cluetrain Manifesto" — 95 theses, nailed to the virtual door of the Web, which contend that because of the Internet, businesses, companies and corporations can't fake it anymore.

Established businesses that support the status quo will find it disturbing. Entrepreneurs and guerrilla marketers who thrive in changing markets will find it stimulating. The Wall Street Journal calls the manifesto "pretentious, strident and absolutely brilliant."

The title? "Because an employee at a formerly-hot company once said: 'The cluetrain stopped there four times a day for ten years and they never took delivery,'" explains Christopher Locke, editor/publisher of Entropy Gradient Reversals.

Locke is one of the ringleaders of the Cluetrain Manifesto, along with Rick Levine, Web architect for Sun Microsystems' Java Software group; Doc Searls, senior editor for Linux Journal; and David Weinberger, editor of JOHO (Journal of the Hyperlinked Organization) They've spent a lot of late nights "talking about what we think is going on in business. Beneath the surface. Even beneath the Web," according to Locke.

The Internet has created a "powerful global conversation," they say. Markets have become so networked, that customers know more about the products than the companies that produce them. The solution is for companies to strip down corporate firewalls and address their markets honestly in a genuine human voice.

"These markets are conversations. Their members communicate in language that is natural, open, honest, direct, funny and often shocking. Whether explaining or complaining, joking or serious, the human voice is unmistakably genuine. It can't be faked.

"... learning to speak in a human voice is not some trick," write the ringleaders of the Cluetrain Manifesto. "Most corporations, on the other hand, only know how to talk in the soothing, humorless monotone of the mission statement, marketing brochure, and your-call-is-important-to-us busy signal. Same old tone, same old lies."

Here's a smattering of theses:

Thesis # 7. "Hyperlinks subvert hierarchy."

Thesis # 15. "In just a few more years, the current homogenized "voice" of business—the sound of mission statements and brochures—will seem as contrived and artificial as the language of the 18th century French court."

Thesis # 74. "We are immune to advertising. Just forget it."

Thesis # 78. "You want us to pay? We want you to pay attention."

The Cluetrain Manifesto isn't just about the relationship between companies and their markets, it's also about the relationship between companies and their employees.

It warns against top-down intranets installed to distribute HR and other information that overlook the potential for an "intranetworked conversation" that engages individuals. It warns that command and control are "poisonous" notions, that "paranoia kills conversations...[and] lack of open conversation kills companies."

Sounds like a bunch of refugees from the late 60's free speech movement, doesn't it? A wave of nostalgia for the passionate idealism of my youth washed over me as I read.

And yet these 30-(?), 40- and 50-somethings are grownups now. They aren't idealistic kids. Perhaps they grew up with their idealism intact, but refined by prolonged exposure to reality.

"If you only have time for one clue his year, this is the one to get...we are not seats or eyeballs or end users or consumers. We are human beings — and our reach exceeds your grasp. Deal with it."

When you've read, marked, learned, and inwardly digested this manifesto, the writers want you to pass it on. Then go to Clues you can Use for pointers on how to dive into this new kind of conversation: hire a historian, burn your mission statement, and cancel casual Fridays are some of them.

You can even post your own clues, if you have some to offer.

Cluetrain Manifesto (http://www.cluetrain.com/)
Ringleaders (http://www.cluetrain.com/ringleaders.html)
buzz (http://www.cluetrain.com/buzz.html)

"...we are not seats or eyeballs or end users or consumers. We are human beings— and our reach exceeds your grasp. Deal with it."

Web Voyeurs Find Intellectual Stimulation

Power users on the Web are justly proud of their ability to find what they want, when they need it, without wasting time.

Occasionally though, it's a relief to put yourself at the mercy of the Internet and go where it leads you. One way to do that is to visit one of the Internet 'voyeur' sites. No, I'm not recommending X-rated content here.

Voyeur sites show you real searches other people are currently conducting. If one sounds interesting (and you've got a fast mouse finger) you can click on it and see the results.

A couple of years ago, the Magellan Internet Guide pioneered this odd entertainment, displaying a list of a dozen or so actual Internet searches as they were being conducted. The list changes every 15 seconds, if your browser permits. That's pretty fast. On a recent visit, searchers were investigating the Foucalt pendulum, the Morgantown Chamber of Commerce, Turkish historical costumes, British Telcom, Sir Isaac Newton — obviously it was a school day.

Naturally there were the people looking for naughty sites, but I was struck by their frequently poor spelling. Unless the purveyors of porno can't spell either, I'm afraid they will be frustrated in their searches. Poor things.

WebCrawler Search Voyeur is another site where you can look over the shoulders of Web searchers, if your browser supports Java. A miniature screen appears in the middle of your monitor, and words scroll across it like a stock market price ticker. Again, you have to be quick on the mouse to catch a search that interests you and click it to see the results. Often enough I find myself looking at results for the next search.

People were investigating Amelia Earhart, crop circles, child custody laws in Colorado, American slavery economics, herring roe, Beanie Babies, Lakota Ghost dances, Widespread Panic, archetypes in literature, bead work, divorce, Monica jokes, and PERL programming.

The archetypes in literature search led me to a fascinating variant on the Tarot fortune-telling system. The Archetypes Storytelling Cards site lets you click a button to display a card or series of cards that you can use as the basis for a game or a story. Writers needing a little jump-start

Naturally there were people looking for naughty sites, but I was struck by their frequently poor spelling.

with their character development or plot might find inspiration here. Of course, you could use it as a basis for meditation or to tell your fortune, if you like.

Magellan users asked questions such as "What is the newest medicine for Crohn's disease?" "Is hypnosis real or fake?" "How do fridges work?" "How do I write a demand payment letter?" and "Are criminals made or born?" Someone wanted to know "how to prepare a Manhattan."

I clicked on the letter question and found Scott Pakin's automatic complaint letter generator. It's a gem.

If you've ever felt upset about someone and can't quite find the words to express yourself, Scott is there to help. Just enter the name of the offender and the number of paragraphs you want, and click a button. Some brief excerpts:

- "Ms. X's shenanigans run on pure irony."
- "I unequivocally feel that her publicity stunts are a pitiful jumble of incoherent nonsense."
- "...let me explain that Mr. Y can't relate to anyone other than the worst kinds of conniving knee-biters there are."
- "You are, I'm sure, well aware that she is as quasi-ignominious as she is bleeding-heart."

Most satisfying, even if you never send a letter.

Someone was searching for info on the "periodic table," another on "crab boil." Someone else wanted a foliage report for New Hampshire, another wanted the National Book Award archive, and still another was researching wholesale yo-yo manufacturers.

As for privacy, WebCrawler claims that they receive "over 5 million queries a day, making it impossible for anyone, WebCrawler staff included, to make the association between a particular search and the person who initiated it."

Magellan (http://www.mckinley.com/)
Magellan Search Voyeur (http://voyeur.mckinley.com/cgi-bin/voyeur.cgi)
WebCrawler (http://webcrawler.com/)
WebCrawler Search Voyeur (http://webcrawler.com/SearchTicker.html)
Archetypes Storytelling Cards (http://www.thecards.com/)
Automatic Complaint Letter Generator (http://www-csag.cs.uiuc.edu/individual/pakin/complaint)

If you've ever felt upset about someone and can't quite find the words to express yourself, Scott is there to help.

Rube Goldberg Alive & Well Online

Ever suffered through the indignities of trying to install (and configure) computer software for an Internet (or Intranet) connection and found yourself wondering just who it was who dreamed up this 'Rube Goldberg' contraption?

Ever wondered what or who a 'Rube Goldberg' is or was?

If you've had personal experience with computers — in the office or at home — you can appreciate the humor and insight of the Pulitzer Prize-winning cartoonist Reuben Lucius Goldberg whose whimsical insights into modern inventions earned him a place in our vocabulary.

Goldberg (1883–1970) began his cartoonist career in 1904 satirizing complex inventions that were supposed to save time and increase efficiency. For the next half century his drawings illustrated machines that were a "symbol of man's capacity for exerting maximum effort to achieve minimal results." He died before computers invaded the workplace but his creative intellect was way ahead of us all.

Fortunately for those too young to have ever seen his cartoons in current newspapers, examples have been posted on the Official Rube Goldberg Website. Analyze such charming inventions as:

... his drawings illustrated machines that were a "symbol of man's capacity for exerting maximum effort to achieve minimal results."

- the Self Operating Napkin, which not only wipes your chin but, with a harmonica substituted for the napkin, allows you to entertain your guests with music after dinner
- the Device for Helping Late Commuters, which relies on the agility of a polar bear scalded by the water boiling over from your car's radiator cap
- the process to Fish an Olive Out of a Long-Necked Bottle, which begins with a weight being dropped on a cigar-smoking dwarf

You think these inventions unlikely? Anyone who has tried to generate a single label or print out an envelope on a laser printer knows exactly what a Rube Goldberg contraption is all about. (Or perhaps your office is one of those which maintains a typewriter just for envelopes?)

Goldberg's inventions not only live on in our cultural psyche, they are also the inspiration for the annual Rube Goldberg Machine Contest sponsored by the professional engineering fraternity, Theta Tau, at Purdue University. The contest, which ran locally from 1949 to 1955, was revived in 1983 and five years later went national.

The contest now receives coverage from such national media as Good Morning America, The Today Show, The Tonight Show and Late Night with David Letterman.

For engineers it's serious stuff. These college students compete to come up with devices that complete a simple task in the most complex way. In previous years teams have been challenged to put a stamp on an envelope, screw in a light bulb, make a cup of coffee — all in 20 or more steps.

One year a team of aerospace engineers from the University of Texas at Austin won the national contest (in 35 steps) with a device that included golf balls, an electric screwdriver, an old guitar and a live rat, and required a pit stop to change tires.

Their challenge? — to load a CD into a CD player.

Contest Rules, Judging Instructions, Tips on How to Build a Rube Machine and suggestions for How to Start a Local Contest are all available online. The local contests are held in February. The National Contest is held in early April.

Contestants the following year were asked to Turn Off An Alarm Clock in <u>more</u> than 20 steps.

If you think that ought to be easy, consider that Rube himself took less than 10 steps with his device for No More Oversleeping: "When sun comes up, magnifying glass (A) burns hole in paper bag (B), dropping water into ladle (C) and lifting gate (D), which allows heavy ball (E) to roll down chute (F) — Rope (G) lifts bed (H) into vertical position and drops you into your shoes (I)... PS: You can't go back and sneak a few winks because there's no place to lie down."

Stay tuned. Some of the brightest minds in the country are focused on this task.

Official Rube Goldberg WebSite (http://www.rube-goldberg.com/rg2idx.htm)
Rube Golderb Inventions (http://www.rube-goldberg.com/card5.gif)
Rube Goldberg Machine Contest (http://www.purdue.edu/UNS/rube/rube.index.html)
Univ. of Texas Winning Device (http://www.purdue.edu/UNS/html4ever/970405.Rube.natl.html)
No More Oversleeping (http://www.rube-goldberg.com/card1.gif)

Contestants were being asked to Turn Off An Alarm Clock in more than 20 steps.

Wacky Sites Help Us Regain Perspective

Sometimes we all need to kick back and relax.

You can run the engine with the throttle wide open for only so long before you jump the track, burn out your tubes, exhaust your weary fireman or finally blow your stack.

It's at times like this that we need to look at the world a little differently, and ponder some of the wacky, weird or bizarre events that take place in the world when we're too focused on our own daily concerns to notice.

Try starting at author Joey Green's "Wacky Uses" Website which showcases wacky uses for, and weird facts about, common household products.

Green is a former advertising copywriter who developed an obsession with the off-beat. He didn't just kick back for a break from the rat race. He quit it; said farewell to the rats; and hiked around the world for two years.

He has spent the past decade writing books about this stuff and his Website is not only an advertising and promotional tool for bookselling but a motherlode of wacky information that may or may not be useful to you one day.

... his Website is not only an advertising and promotional tool for bookselling but a motherlode of wacky information...

Consider, under Wacky Uses:
* Alka-Seltzer: Clean a toilet. Drop in two Alka-Seltzer tablets, wait 20 minutes, brush and flush ...
* Bounce: Collect cat hair. Rubbing a sheet of Bounce will magnetically attract all those loose hairs ...
* Coca-Cola: Clean corrosion from battery terminals. Pour a can of carbonated Coca-Cola over the terminals to bubble away the corrosion ...
* Maxwell House Coffee: Cover spots on black suede. Sponge on a little black Maxwell House coffee ...

Under Weird Facts, wouldn't you love to tell your friends that:
* Although Crisco appears solid, it actually contains 80% liquid oil... suspended in the lattice of fat solids much like honey is held in a honeycomb ...
* When famed money-manager Peter Lynch saw his wife bringing L'eggs panty hose home from the supermarket his fund bought stock in Hanes ... the value rose nearly 600%...

• In 1994 Hormel produced the five billionth can of Spam; laid end to end, five billions cans of Spam would circle the earth 12.5 times.

Green offers links to Amazon.com to buy his books which have such catchy titles as "Polish Your Furniture with Panty Hose," "Paint Your House with Powdered Milk," and "Wash Your Hair with Whipped Cream."

If this has only whetted your appetite you'll want to visit Chuck Shepherd's "News of The Weird" Website which offers archives from the popular syndicated columnist who re-reports stories that are equally wacky and weird.

For instance there was the young man in Prestonburg, KY who shot himself in the left shoulder with a .22 rifle "to see how it felt." The police found him screaming in pain. Ten months later the ambulance was called back to his home. He had shot himself again, in the left shoulder.

There are thousands of these stories and, yes, Shepherd also has books available from Amazon.com.

If you aren't yet ready to believe that truth is stranger than fiction, try Randy Cassingham's "This is True" Website where he offers selections from his weekly syndicated column. You can sign up for the weekly email delivery of the column if your local paper doesn't carry it and, natch, you can also order the books.

Cassingham takes brief snippets from major news sources and adds his own wry comments that are often better than the original material.

For instance: If It's For Me, I'm Not In — Zach Williams, 18, was robbed in Chattanooga, Tenn. He tried to run away and was shot to death. One of the things the robbers stole: his pager. Police, upon learning about the beeper, figured "why not?" and sent it a page. When the murderers returned the cops' call, it was traced to George Morgan, 19, and his cousin Antonio Morgan, 18, who were arrested and charged with murder. (AP)

— Bit by bit, Darwin is being proved right.

Wacky Uses (http://www.wackyuses.com)
News of The Weird Archives (http://www.nine.org/notw/archives.html)
This Is True (http://www.thisistrue.com)

... such catchy titles as "Polish Your Furniture with Panty Hose," "Paint Your House with Powdered Milk," and "Wash Your Hair with Whipped Cream."

Dow Jones Introduces Business Site 'Webliography'

Is it a good thing that anyone can publish anything on the Internet? It's an important question among major players and it goes beyond pornography or libel.

Establishment types are often opposed to the unregulated energies that threaten to overturn the status quo. Champions of competition generally applaud new freedoms and opportunities. But what are we — the consumers — to think?

Is the Internet our ally or enemy?

With an industry evolving as fast as the Net it's hard to tell whether we should favor unknown challengers or rally behind old champions. It's crucial in business to get credible information quickly. But how do you tell whether the latest information published on the Net is legit?

Into this debate now enters one of the 900-lb gorillas of the news business: Dow Jones, publisher of the Wall Street Journal, the company whose name has become almost synonymous with stock market news.

Dow Jones is not debating the issue; it is demonstrating its abilities by producing the Dow Jones Business Directory, a free searchable database of business sites that includes not only links to business resources but reviews of what's actually useful.

Their stated goal is to help users save time while gathering information from reliable and respected sources. If nothing else, that's a worthy ambition that will attract anyone who's ever tried to find information online.

The Dow Jones people have a reputation for gathering business information, making sense of it and organizing it for presentation in a larger context. The DJBD combines their expertise with computer technology to give us what one reviewer aptly describes as a "Webliography" of business sites.

DJ says it uses "site sweeping technology" to keep current and that sounds cutting-edge trendy. More valuable, however, is the small army of editors who actually put human eyeballs on the sites reviewed and then sign their names to their words.

It's crucial in business to get credible information quickly. But how do you tell whether the latest information published on the Net is legit?

Users can search by industry, companies or publications for specific reference or they can cruise general categories like Careers, Companies in the Dow, Economy, Financial Markets, Government, Law, Personal Finance, or Small Businesses.

For instance, the Websites of all of the 30 companies that make up the DJIA are reviewed, from Allied Signal to Walt Disney.

DJBD Reviewer Grace Lichtenstein, cruising the Alcoa site, notes "we found a genuinely intriguing page about how quickly aluminum cans are recycled in our reduce-reuse-recycle culture."

The Coca-Cola site is singled out by Molly Shapiro for being "a hangout for the screenager generation" which "takes hipness to new and sometimes annoying levels."

The Eastman Kodak company gains kudos for its design but also gets a plug for its Picture Network service which allows consumers (at $4.95/month) to upload their own photos as email postcards to be sent online.

The editors say they add 10 to 20 new sites each week in addition to updating reviews of existing sites and maintaining daily news briefs. That means we can look forward to perhaps 750 new business Website reviews each year: a powerful tool that keeps getting more powerful.

There's a certain amount of self-promotion and puffery here, to be sure. Sites that are included are notified by the editors that they've been "chosen" as a DJBD "Select Site" and are thus eligible to post the "award" logo.

That, of course, increases visibility for the DJBD. (One hand washes the other as the proverb puts it.)

What's most useful for consumers however, is a growing database of information on businesses that is developed, maintained, and updated by one of the premier gatekeepers in the business news business.

Dow Jones Business Directory (http://www.bd.dowjones.com)
Companies of the Dow (http://www.bd.dowjones.com/category.asp?CatID=2)

... a growing database of information on businesses that is developed, maintained, and updated by one of the premier gatekeepers in the business news business.

TheStreet.Com Rates the Business Century

As the century draws to a close people everywhere are capitalizing on the universal desire for a summing up, a sense of perspective, an explanation of what it is we've been through.

If you had to name the most important business events or developments of the past century could you come up with a sizable list that your colleagues would agree on? Could you come up with a hundred?

The staff of TheStreet.com — the online financial news source that is chewing on Wall Street Journal turf — has come up with a highly subjective, often irreverent, occasionally witty list that gives a good starting place to judge the forces that have bent us into our present course.

With no lack of modesty they have claimed their picks offer "The Basics of Business History" and perhaps they do. They certainly offer a starting point. You can follow the countdown from number 100 (the founding in 1910 of Hallmark Cards and the beginning of the commercialization of holidays) all the way down to what they judge to be the most important (... I won't spoil it for you).

There are five sections of "signal points, inventions, ideas and companies" you can review to help you get a fix on what's been affecting business over the past century.

Some signal points seem silly — like "Disneyland Opens, July 17, 1955" — until you read that it opened with Ronald Reagan hosting a live special broadcast on ABC; that it was the first major destination theme park in the world, that Disney's parks are now a $5 billion-a-year business and that Disney World in Orlando with 50,000 employees is the "largest single-site employer in the US." Okay. That rates a mention.

How about "AOL goes to flat-rate pricing: Oct. 29, 1996"? I had to ponder that long and hard. I'm guessing it's a good choice that will become more apparent as time passes. You only have to look at Europe where the Internet has been slow to take off because they don't even have flat-rate pricing on basic telephone service.

The launch of Federal Express in April, 1973 got my attention because it not only revolutionized essential business deliveries, it gave the Post Office a good kick in the butt which seems to have almost pushed the old federal pensioner into being a profitable competitor. (You also have to ask yourself if venture capitalists would have taken e-commerce proposals seriously if the pony-tailed entrepreneurs had planned to deliver their products by mail.)

... a highly subjective, often irreverent, occasionally witty list ...

Bill Hewlett and Dave Packard's 1939 launch of their electronics business in a shed in what was to become Silicon Valley doesn't seem pivotal until you learn that "$5 billion — or a third of all venture capital raised in the world — is invested in Silicon Valley..." Then it seems pivotal. Way pivotal.

As you get into the top ten there is little question about the importance: Carrier Engineering's 1915 launch of commercial air conditioning? Right.

Henry Ford's 1913 assembly line production? Okay.

Intel's 1971 invention of the micro-chip? You bet.

The great Stock Market Crash of 1929? With the sobering reflection that between October '29 and July '32 the market lost 89% of its value and didn't recover to 1929 levels until November '54, you'd have to say this is a definite contender.

If you want to cut to the bottom line (old-fashioned business training) you can look at the Numerical List. For a more studied approach, try the Chronological List.

If you don't agree with their selections, the editors invite your contributions. See Reader Feedback for a sample of those who've already vented.

Personally I thought that medical innovations, including the discovery of penicillin and insulin, the introduction of birth control pills, the eradication of smallpox, the invasion of AIDS and the prolonging of the average life span were all much more important to business than many of TSC's nominees.

I would also have listed the Marshall Plan for the reconstruction of war-torn Europe right up there with the Atomic Bomb, the income tax alongside the minimum wage, the invention of the office copier alongside the abandoning of carbon paper, the federally imposed integration of schools alongside the emergence of English as a global language — all of which were omitted.

TheStreet.com (http://www.thestreet.com)
The Basics of Business History (http://www.thestreet.com/basics/countdown/747895.html)
Numerical List (http://www.thestreet.com/basics/countdown/747965.html)
Chronological List (http://www.thestreet.com/basics/countdown/748433.html)
Reader Feedback (http://www.thestreet.com/basics/countdown/747986.html)

If you don't agree with their selections, the editors invite your contributions.

Web Reveals Competitive Intelligence

The capture of the top-secret, electro-mechanical encryption machine known as "Enigma" — and the subsequent cracking of enemy codes used by the German high command to communicate with field commanders — gave the Allies in World War II a distinct advantage from the very early days of that dreadful conflict.

Time and again, especially before America joined the war, when tiny Britain stood alone against the seemingly invincible might of the victorious Axis powers, critical intelligence allowed weaker and smaller Allied forces to mass their strength against vastly superior numbers and prevail.

It may be fashionable now to say that the forces of good triumphed over evil in that bitter struggle a half century ago but, as any modern business product manager well appreciates, it helps immeasurably to have your competitor's play book and know his plans in advance.

Although business is not war and the competition is not the enemy, the struggle for profits in the marketplace resonates with the metaphors of battle. Nowhere is this more noticeable than in the quest for business intelligence.

In the Age of Information the hunter-gatherer culture is still predominant and those with skills in hunting and gathering intelligence from out of the datasmog are in high demand.

Their services are not just restricted to large multi-national corporations either. The Web now provides resources for the little guy that can even the playing field more than just a little.

If you've never even considered the value of competitive intelligence start with The Society of Competitive Intelligence Professionals' Website. The society has more than 6,000 members from 53 countries and they exchange information regularly. Visit the ongoing chat forums and listen in on their discussions.

If you're curious about how you can mine the Internet for competitive intelligence see the forum discussion in Fast Company magazine in which Associate Editor Gina Imperato got professionals to reveal such tips as:

- using the search engine Deja News, which tracks discussion groups, to discover that a privately held company had recently posted 14 job openings — a key indication of development strategy

... it helps immeasurably to have your competitor's play book and know his plans in advance.

- compiling information from corporate Web pages as well as hometown newspapers to build a profile of company managers that will let you understand whether they're marketers, cost cutters, visionaries, penny-pinchers, etc.
- track industry conference sites where keynote speeches are often posted, giving you insights into the star talent at individual companies
- analyze help wanted ads at sites such as CareerPath and The Monster Board to see what kind of technical background individual companies seek from new hires

If all this poking around has whetted your appetite you might want to visit the massive Competitive Intelligence Guide maintained by Fuld & Company, the 20-year-old Boston company which has set the standards for much of the industry.

Start with Fuld's Corporate Evaluation Questionnaire: 40 probing and prodding questions that will rattle your complacency about your business no matter how big (or small) you are.

Want to scout out the sources yourself? Look at Fuld's Internet Intelligence Index: links to more than 600 Websites "covering everything from macro-economic data to individual patent and stock quote information."

If you're just looking for some trendy jargon to drop into the next staff meeting scan Fuld's Intelligence Dictionary. There you'll find such beauts as Cost Drivers, Gap Analysis, and my favorite: Humint — "short hand expression, meaning Human Intelligence..."

Enigma (http://www.twintrees.demon.co.uk/minfo.html)
Society of Competitive Intelligence Professionals (http://www.scip.org)
Forum Discussion in Fast Company (http://www.fastcompany.com/online/14/intelligence.html)
Deja News (http://www.dejanews.com)
CareerPath (http://www.careerpath.com)
The Monster Board (http://www.monsterboard.com)
Competitive Intelligence Guide (http://www.fuld.com)
Fuld's Corporate Evaluation Questionnaire (http://www.fuld.com/StrategiesCorpEval.html)
Fuld's Internet Intelligence Index (http://www.fuld.com/i3/index.html)
Fuld's Intelligence Dictionary (http://www.fuld.com/Dictionary/index.html)

... 40 probing and prodding questions that will rattle your complacency about your business no matter how big (or small) you are.

Web Immigrants Throng Library of Congress

The **Library** of CONGRESS

... requests exceeded two million per month in 1995, eight million/month a year later, 25 million/month in '97 ... and it topped 56 million at the close of '99

When I was a child, asking a question that showed gross ignorance or lack of attention was often answered derisively with "What? You just got off the boat?"

This was often delivered with a mock foreign accent which indicated (1) offensive prejudice about immigrants, and (2) that at some deeper level the culture recognized that we were almost universally a nation of immigrants.

I am repeatedly struck by the recollection as I tour the shifting shores of the Web where we are all immigrants all the time. How do I find..? Where do I go for..? Who might have..?

If you're looking for government information in the United States you owe it to yourself to start at the Library of Congress. You don't have to go to Washington. You don't have to apply for permission. You don't have to wait in line.

This extraordinary resource, once envisioned as a handy tool for Congressmen (and once consisting entirely of Thomas Jefferson's personal library of 6,487 books), is now online in such abundance that you almost need a tour guide to understand what's available. And it's expanding all the time. (Not only is the information growing but the use of it is expanding correspondingly. The number of requests exceeded two million per month in 1995, eight million/month a year later, 25 million/month in '97, 47 million/month in '98 and it topped 56 million/month at the close of '99.)

The site opens with a simple array of sites that includes links to seven major areas:

• American Memory: superb collections of exhibits that "tell America's story" from Baseball Cards to Historic Preservation
• THOMAS: the full text of current legislation under consideration by the Congress.
• Exhibitions: the online archive of exhibits that have been open to the public in Washington, DC.
• Using the Library: catalogs, collections and research services.
• Library Today: news, events.
• Copyright Office: forms and information
A sidebar links to Help & FAQs; general information

But don't be fooled by the simplicity of what's offered. Most of what's available is not apparent. It's not hidden, it's just fiendishly organized.

For instance, if you want to get a handle, so to speak, on what kind of information might be online for the Executive branch of the government try this:

(1) From the Opening Page click on Using the Library; this will take you to the Collections and Services Page.

(2) Under Collections, click on Reading Rooms & Centers and then drop down to click on the hyperlinked "Newspaper and Current Periodical" line.

(3) At the Newspaper & Periodical Reading Room go over to the left and click on "Government Publications." (Please stay with me; you'll pass scores of other interesting sites but we really are going somewhere.)

(4) At Government Publications you'll find "Bibliographies and Guides;" halfway down the list click on "Official Federal Government Websites."

(5) Voila! The page opens with all the Websites for the Executive Branch and eventually winds up with links to the Judicial and Legislative Branches after offering links to everything from the White House to The Smithsonian Institution and in between.

Of course, if you knew the exact wording of what you wanted you could use the Search/Browse function from the opening page and get a list of possible hits. That saves a lot of time if you do know exactly what you want but you miss out on an awful lot of serendipitous discovery along the way.

You want to know what's available at the Library of Congress? Look it up online.

You don't know how to look it up online? What? You just got off the boat? Go to their "Explore the Internet" site; it makes it even easier.

Library of Congress (http://loc.gov/)
Using the Library (http://www.loc.gov/library/)
Reading Rooms (http://lcweb.loc.gov/rr/rrbrief.html)
Research and Reference (http://loc.gov/rr/research.html)
Newspaper & Periodical Reading Room (http://lcweb.loc.gov/rr/news)
Government Publications (http://lcweb.loc.gov/rr/news/lcgovd.html)
Official Federal Government Web Sites (http://lcweb.loc.gov/global/executive/fed.html)
Explore the Internet (http://lcweb.loc.gov/global/explore.html)

Most of what's available is not apparent. It's not hidden, it's just fiendishly organized.

Inflation Calculators Offer Perspective

Inflation can be more destructive than any amount of bombs lobbed or dropped by an enemy.

Inflation became a topic of adult conversation when I was a teenager.

I had been introduced to the concept in my own world as the five-cent Coke and nickel candy bar doubled in price and then continued to either climb in price or shrink in size or both. Adults saw it on a much larger scale.

The elders on the porch nodded sagely and recalled family lore. Great-grandfather, they said, used to recount that before the War he went to market with money in his pocket and brought back food in a basket but at the end of the War the equation was reversed.

The War, in their case, was the one that lasted from 1861 to 1865, referred to in textbooks as The Civil War, sometimes called The War between the States, occasionally referred to on the porch as The War of Northern Aggression.

The name doesn't really matter. War exacts the same penalty on the losers in any conflict. Inflation can be more destructive than any amount of bombs lobbed or dropped by an enemy.

It's the chief bugaboo of Federal Reserve economists and particularly its chairman, Alan Greenspan, who broadly hints at increased interest rates as pre-emptive strikes at potential inflationary trends.

On the other hand, with record economic growth and unparalleled increases in productivity, some economists are now actually discussing the possibility of deflation: an economic phenomenon unseen by anyone in the current generation.

What's a body to think?

Fortunately the power of the Internet makes the intelligent discussion of inflation a topic any family can pursue. Start at The Inflation Calculator created by Morgan Friedman, a recent graduate of the UPenn. This simple tool adjusts the value of money according to inflation based on the Consumer Price Index from 1800 to 1998.

Consider for instance, my great-grandfather who lived from 1833 to 1916. According to Friedman's calculator a dollar in 1833 had a value of $1.01 in 1916 dollars. Inflation was almost non-existent during my great-grandfather's lifetime (not counting the years during "The War" he was talking about).

My grandfather lived from 1874 to 1930. A dollar in 1874 would have had the purchasing power of 70 cents in 1930. He knew something of the power of inflation to erode a dollar's value.

My father, who was born in 1915, has seen a world of inflation in his lifetime. The 1915 dollar was worth only six cents in 1998 — the most recent year for which figures are available. Put another way, that 1915 dollar would have had $15.90 in 1998-dollar purchasing power.

In my own lifetime, nearing half a century, inflation has been both up and down, the dollar of 1950 being worth only 15 cents in 1998 terms.

When you take the raw numbers and plug them in to your own family's experience the pocket and basket analogy not only make much more sense but the whole global argument begins to come into focus.

If you're interested in more detail try the Consumer Price Index Inflation Calculator maintained by NASA, the space agency. Their figures only go back to 1913 but you can quickly calculate that inflation since then has been 1546%!

If you'd like to investigate historical periods of deflation try the Current Value of Old Money Website maintained by the distinguished British Academic Roy Davies. He offers Global Financial Data back to the year 1264 — yes, more than 700 years of English consumer prices with a base of 100 set in 1275.

England's economy offers an extraordinary example of deflation from about 1920 to 1940 when prices began to rise and the value of money began to erode. Inflation doubled from 1940 to 1950, increased another 50% by 1960, another 80% by 1970, and jumped a whopping 400% between 1970 and 1980; it had doubled again by 1993.

Are we headed for inflation or deflation? The past don't predict the future but, looking back, you can certainly get a new perspective on the dangers that economists are talking about.

The Inflation Calculator (http://www.westegg.com/inflation)
Consumer Price Index Inflation Calculator (http://www.jsc.nasa.gov/bu2/inflateCPI.html)
Current Value of Old Money (http://www.exeter.ac.uk/~RDavies/aria/current/howmuhc.html)
Global Financial Data (http://www.globalfindata.com/tbukcpi.htm)

In my own lifetime, nearing half a century, inflation has been both up and down, the dollar of 1950 being worth only 15 cents in 1998 terms.

Cut Through the Data-smog with BizProWeb

The never-ending search for Websites that offer information that is both timely and useful can often seem like the quest for the Holy Grail.

We have been led to believe that the answer to everything is online. Those who have been involved in the quest are all too aware that may be true and that is the problem — not the solution.

How do you cut through the data-smog to find what you're looking for when so much is available?

The answer is the same as that given to any traveler in a foreign country: find a good guide.

If you're looking for business information online one of the most helpful guides around is Craig Sonnenberg, editor of the huge and growing BizProWeb.

Sonnenberg has developed a "virtual library of business resources" which is "targeted toward the needs of small business owners, professionals, and other home office entrepreneurs."

In the classic Web strategy of providing value through aggregating the offerings of others, BizProWeb now offers almost 700 pages of business links and resources.

In the classic Web strategy of providing value through aggregating the offerings of others, BizProWeb now offers almost 700 pages of business links and resources.

The site opens with Picks of the Day — daily recommendations for new sites, shareware and newsgroups of specific interest to business. This is worth a daily visit just to find out what's new that's useful. (If you can only get by once a week you can go back and see previous picks you've missed.)

The collection of recommended Websites is a superb resource simply because it has organized other Websites into 22 subject categories which are immediately accessible, ranging from Accounting and Finance to Website Development.

The links to Business and Professional Newsgroups is especially helpful to entrepreneurs who may be choking on the dataglut generated by the more than 20,000 chat groups currently sharing discussions online. BizProWeb has selected almost 1,000 of these newsgroups based on the quality of their content and organized them into two lists: Business and Professional.

If you've never experienced or participated in a newsgroup this is good place to get your feet wet. The Shareware directory provides links to software developers who provide their programs on a "try-before-you-buy" basis. BizProWeb's contribution here is organizing the software by operating system: DOS, Macintosh, Windows 3.1, Windows 95, 98 and Windows NT.

If you're looking for good old-fashioned magazine-style articles about specific business challenges, the Features library offers over 140 articles arranged under 17 broad topics, including such gems as "Using Dirt Cheap Online Market Research to Grow Your Business" by Marty Foley. Each article has information about the author with links to their Websites and email addresses if you want to contact them.

BizProWeb also offers Forums for visitors to post messages about specific topics or problems they're interested in. Forums operate as a sort of peer mentoring group where people around the world freely share their opinions and experience.

The forums are moderated; you have to subscribe to join; commercial messages and vulgar language is prohibited; the moderator will remove inappropriate postings; and participants understand that this is meant to be a place for exchanging ideas that can be of general benefit for all.

Current forums include Small Business, Accounting & Finance, Marketing & Promotion and Home Office. Additional forums may be added as interest in specific topics develops.

Add BizProWeb to your bookmarks; this guide's worth getting to know.

Craig Sonnenberg (http://www.bizproweb.com/pages/about/about.html)
BizProWeb (http://www.bizproweb.com)
Picks of the Day (http://www.bizproweb.com/pages/picks/picks_of_the_day.html)
Business and Professional Web Sites
     (http://www.bizproweb.com/pages/websites/websites_home.html)
Business and Professional Newsgroups
     (http://www.bizproweb.com/pages/newsgroups/newsgroups_home.html)
Shareware (http://www.bizproweb.com/pages/shareware/shareware.html)
Features library (http://www.bizproweb.com/pages/features/features.html)
Forums (http://www.bizproweb.com/pages/forums/index.shtml)

If you've never experienced or participated in a newsgroup this is good place to get your feet wet.

BestCalls Connects Consumers to Conference Calls

"Looks like more information than I need and would lead to a vicious cycle of market research," a friend emailed me back when I sent her the link to BestCalls.com.

She's typical of many small investors who use the Internet for researching stock buys, but don't want to give up their lives to the pursuit. Still, she might eventually change her mind when she gets used to the idea of listening in on the quarterly analyst telephone calls for companies whose stock she owns.

For those of you who don't know about these calls, the site has an explanation.

A conference call, "sometimes referred to as an 'earnings conference call,' a 'quarterly conference call,' or an 'analyst call,' is an event in which investors can call into a special phone number and hear the management of their company comment on the financial results of the recently completed quarter. Most publicly held companies hold four conference calls per year...."

...although 59 percent of all stock assets are controlled by individual investors like my friend, few of them know these calls exist and fewer ask to join in.

"In the past, these calls were only made available to Wall Street analysts and large institutional investors..."

According to Mark Coker, the founder of BestCalls.com, the National Investor Relations Institute found that four out of five publicly traded companies were holding investor conference calls in early 1998, but fewer than a third of them allowed individual investors to participate.

He suggests that this is partly because, although 59 percent of all stock assets are controlled by individual investors like my friend, few of them know these calls exist and fewer ask to join in.

"Typically," he points out in an interview posted at the site, "if an individual investor asks to participate in a call, most companies will allow it."

Through his Website, which officially launched March 22, 1999, Coker is working to open the conference calls to individual investors and to educate and notify them so they can participate.

The services are free and supported by advertising. His target audience includes investors, investor relations professionals, brokers, industry analysts and media.

The core of the site is a directory that tracks call schedules for thousands of publicly traded companies, with telephone numbers, pass codes, replay information and links to audiocasts and articles. Investors or prospective investors can register for automatic email reminders of calls in which they are interested through CallTracker.

When you register and set up a portfolio in CallTracker, you are also linked to additional information about each security you enter a symbol for, including performance charts, news and other information from BigCharts.com.

Coker and his staff rely on visitors to the site for conference call information. "After a member submits a call, the data is reviewed for accuracy and completeness before it is posted," Coker said.

In addition to schedules and notification of conference calls, there are articles about conference calls including tips on etiquette, a glossary, and thoughts on managing conference calls for investor relations professionals.

Under the Links tab, you'll find BestCalls' Portal, an index of links to Websites of interest to investors. There are message boards, charting and research services, financial publications, associations and clubs, news, and investor relations resources. Among the last are several conference call audiocasters. If you don't know what you might be getting into if you join in on one of these conference calls, you can get an idea from c-call.com or the Vcall Website. At either you can listen to public replays and simulcasts of conference calls and other audiocasts, using RealNetwork, Inc.'s RealPlayer. Registration is free at both.

BestCalls.com (http://www.bestcalls.com)
BigCharts.com (http://www.bigcharts.com/)
c-call.com (http://www.c-call.com/)
Vcall (http://www.vcall.com)

The core of the site is a directory that tracks call schedules for thousands of publicly traded companies...

Search Engines Need Your Input before You're Found

If you are serious about positioning your business on the Internet and making big bucks through online commerce, let me be the first to wish you luck. You have lots and lots of competition.

Once you've developed a product or service people want, you've only just begun. A great Website design only takes you a tiny bit further. No matter how wonderful your mousetrap, the world will not beat a path to your door if it can't find your address.

And to have your address found you'll want to be found by the search engines — the address books of the Internet. To find out how they work and how best to take advantage of them, you'll want to see Danny Sullivan's Search Engine Watch.

From an introduction to search engine design to a monthly email newsletter, The Search Engine Report, Sullivan offers an in-depth, constantly updated course. You can learn how to tailor your listing so your site turns up on top when people are looking for what you have to offer.

In A Webmaster's Guide to Search Engines, Sullivan explains the differences between search engines and directories — the former run automatically, the latter are created by humans. Each has value. There is also a list of the major engines and a description of each.

No matter how wonderful your mousetrap, the world will not beat a path to your door if it can't find your address.

He offers design tips and information on various techniques you can use to attract the attention of both engines and directories as well as ways to monitor traffic to your site and additional information of interest.

The site's status reports on various search engines, ranking them by both popularity and efficiency, may be helpful, but some of them are months out of date. Still, once you visit this site, you'll subscribe to the newsletter and stay abreast of new technology, services and other developments that may not have made it to the site.

For example, a recent issue of the newsletter had an interesting analysis of the introduction of paid listings by the major engines and the illusion that a level playing field had existed beforehand:

"Manipulating crawler-based search results is increasingly becoming a sophisticated, industrial-strength affair. Any service that depends on automation for its primary listings is vulnerable to people who will try to outwit their ranking systems," writes Sullivan. "Sites with great content continue to be poorly ranked due to design issues, while some relevant sites get higher placement over other relevant sites simply because their Webmasters know more about search engine optimization."

Search engine positioning is important, but it isn't everything. Bizmove.com, the Small Business Knowledge Base, has a good section on Internet business.

Meir Liraz, CEO of BizMove.com has an article on the basics of starting an online business, with links to online resources and tips.

There are reviews and excerpts from books such as "Winning the Affiliate Game" by Declan Dunn who points out such basic but easily forgotten truths as "sell one thing and sell it well," "get good profit margins," and "don't just display a banner ad and hope for the best."

Jim Daniels of JDD Publishing has a piece on Marketing with Email, which points out up front that untargeted email or "Unsolicited Bulk Email" is both a waste of time and risky. He then goes on to enumerate some successful techniques he's used for targeting email, with links to further information.

There is a lot more here, including email addresses for selected media from NBC Nightly News to Bed & Breakfast Magazine to Minority Business Entrepreneur and tips on making money with reseller programs.

And of course, there's info here on getting top search engine positioning, including a link to Search Engine Watch.

Search Engine Watch (http://www.searchenginewatch.com/)
A Webmaster's Guide to Search Engines
    (http://www.searchenginewatch.com/webmasters/index.html)
Bizmove.com (http://www.bizmove.com/)
Growing a Business on the Internet (http://www.bizmove.com/internet/main.htm)

"Manipulating crawler-based search results is increasingly becoming a sophisticated, industrial-strength affair."

Different Search Engines Yield Different Results

It's no longer possible to count the number of Websites — does that surprise you? With more than one billion of them, ranging from elegant and comprehensive to insignificant and minute, it shouldn't.

It's no surprise either that no one search engine or index comes close to offering a complete catalog of what's out there. If you are looking for something specific and you don't find it, that's no guarantee that it doesn't exist online — somewhere. Even the biggest search engines now resort to sampling.

Don't be discouraged. Here's an analogy: do you worry that with all the books, brochures and pamphlets out there, you may have missed something that's been written on a particular subject? You probably don't, even though you know there are gems out there you'll never find.

Instead you go to your favorite public library or bookstore and look through the volumes the librarians and buyers have collected. They're constrained by time, interests and budgets when making their selections, but someone has sifted through mountains of available stuff and selected things they think you'll want to read.

It's the same with the Internet. Think of the portals and search engines as librarians or buyers. Any one of them will return the high profile big bucks sites — just as you can buy bestsellers just about anywhere, even in the grocery store.

It's when you search the rest of the Web that you'll begin to perceive the differences. As an experiment, run a search using Yahoo!, AltaVista, HotBot and Excite. Each one will come up with different sites.

... no one search engine or index comes close to offering a complete catalog of what's out there.

If you are researching a client or information about a product you should try them all.

Let's say you have a great idea — revive the Pet Rock. What's your competition? Is anyone already there? Are there better ideas?

Enter the words "pet rock" in the space in each search engine, and you will discover that several people are testing the idea. HotBot and Excite both found Bear Rock Productions' Return of the Pet Rock where you can buy one — in your choice of box color — for $5 plus shipping etc.

Excite also found the Virtual Pet site, which has reprinted an article on the history of the fad from the Encyclopedia of POP Culture, by Jane and Michael Stern, Harper Perennial Press 1992. If you need inspiration, the article mentions several other bewildering fads which made their inventors millionaires.

AltaVista returned Jimmy Rocker's Brainstorm, an "idea generation subscription service" to help you come up with your own fad! The site is pretty entertaining — or annoying, depending on your point of view.

Yahoo! found sites about hand painted rocks with images of your pet — not the same thing —and a daily devotional from the Presbyterian Church in Canada titled "My Pet Rock." It's on the Bible verse 1 Samuel 7:12 - "Then Samuel took a stone and set it up. He named it Ebenezer, saying, 'Thus far has the Lord helped us.'"

Now there's a big moneymaker — religious pet rocks.

Don't laugh. Think of the W.W.J.D. phenomenon. If you haven't spotted the jewelry, books, bracelets and other ephemera aimed at teenagers and younger children emblazoned with the acronym for "What Would Jesus Do?" you live a sheltered life. Lucky you.

Each of these search engines also has a "portal" or index which you can use for a more orderly approach to the Web. Links are arranged in categories and all but HotBot have links to breaking news stories as well.

Which is the best? It all depends on what you mean by that. One might be the most comprehensive and still not return the site you're looking for.

Generally I like AltaVista because you can ask it questions in ordinary English as well as search by keywords. However, when AltaVista announced it was considering selling the top two spots on its search results to companies willing to pay the price you should have seen the fur fly on Internet discussion groups.

Most search engines sell ad space on the results page. Selling the results themselves doesn't seem to be an idea whose time has come.

Yahoo! (http://www.yahoo.com)
AltaVista (http://www.altavista.com)
HotBot (http://www.hotbot.com)
Excite (http://www.excite.com)

Enter the words "pet rock" in the space in each search engine, and you will discover that several people are testing the idea.

EgoSurf Never Quits Searching

Great-grandmother gave very good advice when she said your name should only appear in print three times (when you're born, when you're married and when you die).

She never heard radio. She never went to a "talkie." She never saw TV. She never imagined the Internet. To her, privacy was a treasure to be guarded closely; a good name often the only legacy one could bequeath to children as a family struggled out of post-war poverty.

That was then. This is now. Grandmother would undoubtedly be astonished at the lengths to which some people go to get publicity.

As people in business know very well, however, anonymity is death. Building name recognition is essential to every successful enterprise.

It's expensive and time-consuming. It's an art rather than a science. It's also difficult to keep track of. (What's the point of being mentioned if you yourself don't hear about it?)

Numerous ventures have been launched on the Internet to help people keep track of their Web publicity and one of the more ingenious is "EgoSurf" created by InGenius Technologies of Kalamazoo, Michigan.

The premise is simple: you type in your name and EgoSurf will yoke together several of the large search engines to return a list of all Web pages that include your name.

If your name is Bill Clinton you'll probably amass a list of millions of pages, some of which you probably don't want to read. But if you've got a fairly uncommon name you'll probably get a more manageable list.

Obviously this could be fun. Is it useful?

What's the point of being mentioned if you yourself don't hear about it?

Well actually, yes. You can use it to retrieve a list of anyone's name but you can also search for a trademark, a phrase or a string of keywords. For instance, if you've just sent out a press release announcing the invention of "Shockoe Bottom Electric SeatWarmers" you can search for the phrase and find out who has mentioned it and where.

The results are scored and averaged so you can sort them by your own standards of relevance.

How is this different from all the other search engines out there?

First of all, EgoSurf is the Energizer Bunny of search engines. It doesn't quit.

You can leave your email address with EgoSurf and it will continue to send you more matching links as they are discovered.

EgoSurf starts with the fastest search engines and sends you the first dozen results immediately. Overnight it will bring in the results from other search engines. For a full week it will keep on banging the drum, sending you the results.

Second, EgoSurf actually won't inundate you with millions of results if your name is Bill Clinton. According to InGenius Technologies CEO Julie Stock her company has created special search algorithms that continuously filter the Web and return the most relevant results.

"You don't receive every single link," says Stock, "only the best, at most 50 links a day."

Need more than a week's worth of results? You can launch another EgoSurf every week or — and this is, as they say, "Way Hip" — you can use another of InGenius Technologies' little toys, "javElink," to save your search and create a perpetual EgoSurf file.

You go surf...
I go surf...
EgoSurf !

Like EgoSurf, javElink is a free service which allows you to monitor up to 20 Web pages, receiving email notification as they change. If you take the Website address of your EgoSurf results page and copy it into a free javElink account you have created your own perpetual notification service.

How can they make money on this if they give everything away for free you might ask. Good question. The answer lies in their core product, NetBrief, which debuted in late 1998 and is designed for large corporate clients who need a professional level of Web monitoring, profiling and intelligence gathering.

NetBrief is to EgoSurf as a Nuclear Power Plant is to the Energizer Bunny. If you need power you go for the big stuff. In the meantime, the creators have given us some pretty useful tools that aren't just toys.

EgoSurf (http://www.egosurf.com)
InGenius Technologies (http://www.ingetech.com)
javElink (http://www.javelink.com)
NetBrief (http://www.netbrief.com)

NetBrief is to EgoSurf as a Nuclear Power Plant is to the Energizer Bunny.

Whatis.com Keeps Getting Better

Upgrade. Quick! What does the word mean to you?

Do you feel excited and pleased or sick and dreadful?

Many of us who have dealt with computers, software, the Internet and Web for the past decade have lost the original sense of pleasant anticipation and learned to be wary at the very mention of the word.

Every once in a while, however, we revisit a Website and realize that an upgrade has been slipped in unnoticed and what was very good has gotten even better.

A prime example is "whatis.com" — an extraordinary collection of definitions, explanations and references that gives renewed life to that most hackneyed of phrases: a wealth of information.

Originally a kitchen-table project of Lowell, Suzanne, Hillary and Emily Thing trying to get a personal grip on technology terms, whatis.com was launched onto the Internet in September 1996 with 350 plain language definitions of Internet and computer terms.

(We might point out that this is not a typical kitchen table project since Lowell is a former IBM technical writer, wife Suzanne is described as "usability lab coordinator," Hillary is a student of Chinese medicine and Emily is an illustrator and graphics designer.)

The Things added material as they went along. By the end of 1997 the list had grown to more than a thousand definitions, over 5,000 hyperlinked cross-references and 3,000 links to other sites. In mid-1999 site included more than 2,000 topics with more than 12,000 hyperlinks.

The original long alphabetical list early on gave way to a frames version that is cross referenced and can be navigated more easily. Individual, smaller subject lists such as New Technology, Cyberculture, Using the Internet, and Writing HTML, were added. "Learning Paths" were created to read definition topics sequentially.

The Excite search engine was introduced in 1998 for specific subjects and the "whatis.com Search Box" is now available for individuals to use on their own Web pages for immediate look-up.

... gives renewed life to that most hackneyed of phrases: a wealth of information.

A major project resulted in "How the Internet Works" — an illustrated tour that gives anyone a clear understanding of how we connect to each other computer to computer around the globe. Best of all, the tour has hyperlinks to many of the definitions included in the major list.

Contributors from around the world accepted Lowell Thing's offer to treat the site as a collaboration and began to send suggestions and add definitions. (To date they have received more than 7,000 comments from over 50 countries; traffic has grown from 4,500 user sessions per day in '97 to 22,000 at the end of '98 to more than 35,000 in mid-'99.)

Typical is the "Every File Format in the World" collection contributed by Andrew Cray and Reg Harbeck which explains all those esoteric suffixes at the end of computer files.

One of the best additions to whatis.com is the collection of sites modestly named "Handy." This includes links to US Area Codes, calculators, country codes for domain names, currency converter, Internet demographics, email addresses, maps, starting places on the Web, weather forecasts for 3600 cities and ZIP Codes.

Whatis.com offers information both on books they recommend and books recommended by their readers. They also have online forms for adding new words and making suggestions to improve the site.

If you're still a complete NetNovice you'll want to look at "How to use whatis" which is the Things' gentle introduction to the powerful information they've assembled.

If you rate yourself as a fairly advanced Internaut you'll want to look at "Our latest discovery" — the Things' showcase of Websites they're excited about. "Some will be useful," they say, "some will be remarkable to look at and interact with, and others — well, we're not sure."

What we can be sure of is that the constant slow upgrading of whatis.com has built value over the long term. This is an upgrade that restores value to the definition of the word and marks whatis.com as worthy of a permanent bookmark.

whatis.com (http://www.whatis.com)
New Technology (http://www.whatis.com/newtech.htm)
Cyberculture (http://www.whatis.com/cybercul.htm)
Using the Internet (http://www.whatis.com/using.htm)

Typical is the "Every File Format in the World" collection ... which explains all those esoteric suffixes at the end of computer files.

AndoverNet Serves High-Tech Consumers

Listen-up tech-junkies! Here's a site that will make you want to get out your cotton swabs and rubbing alcohol and polish up your mouseball.

AndoverNet is an ambitious project that offers free Internet tools, services and links to the latest news stories about major technology issues.

If you're addicted to finding out what's going on with technology and determined to stay up to speed you'll want to bookmark AndoverNet right away. Better yet, sign up for their free email newsletter and have the news come to you.

Andover News Network currently breaks technology news into nine "Watch" categories: Apple, Hardware, Internet, IT, Java, Microsoft, Netscape, Software and Telco.

If you're addicted to finding out what's going on with technology and determined to stay up to speed you'll want to bookmark AndoverNet right away.

Click on HardwareWatch, for instance, and you'll find the latest breaking news on computer hardware from the past week, arranged by date and time. You can sort by topic or alphabetically. You can also extend the date range if you want to find everything, say, that's been written about a topic since last August. Of course, there's also a search engine for keywords.

Hey, this is handy even for non-techno-wonks. Just plain useful.

A tip of the old eye-shade to the Web page designers: if you click on their icon of a double-box, your browser will open the news story in a new window; you won't lose your place on the AndoverNet page. That's a courtesy that more Websites are beginning to extend.

Among the tools AndoverNet offers is the Internet Traffic Report. It measures performance of different Internet routers every hour and gives a simple stoplight report: you know, green means go, yellow means slow down, red means stop. It also gives a numeric value: 100 being the absolute best, zero being the worst. On a recent check we found the rating at 63 in mid afternoon: not bad but not exactly screaming. Most routers were normal. A few rated as slow. One Canadian service rated as bad but they'd just had that awful ice storm and either everyone was on the Internet checking on each other or all their connections were down.

Does this mean anything to you if you're just an average Internet user? Well, it might help you feel a little better if you know it's not just you or your inadequate computer that's causing Internet delays. Check here to find out if your problem is local or global.

Other services offered by AndoverNet include:

- "Cool Tool of the Day" — a review of "essential, cutting edge software;" you can also browse previous reviews by keyword, category or platform.
- "Dave Central" — a mammoth collection of reviews of Windows software, including download addresses for more than 2,500 products.
- "Free Code" — yep, this is where you can get computer code to write a lot of those cool programs you see on other people's Web sites. This is like a candy store for the propeller-heads. Yum.
- "MediaBuilder" — a collection of software, online tools, search engines, and huge library of free images you can use to build your own Website.
- "Slaughterhouse" — regularly updated reviews and comparisons of Windows software including reviews by users like you. Go ahead, submit one yourself.

If you're a high-tech consumer AndoverNet should rate a permanent bookmark. If you're just curious you owe yourself at least one visit.

AndoverNet (http://www.andover.net)
HardwareWatch (http://www.HardwareWatch.com/index.html?an000en_andanavbar)
Internet Traffic Report (http://www.andovernews.com/trafficreport.html?at000en_andanavbar)
Cool Tool of the Day (http://www.CoolTool.com/index.html?at000en_andanavbar)
Dave Central (http://www.HardwareWatch.com/index.html?ann000en_andanavbar)
Free Code (http://www.FreeCode.com/index.html?at000en_andanavbar)
MediaBuilder (http://www.MediaBuilder.com/index.html)
Slaughterhouse (http://www.SlaughterHouse.com/index.html?at000en_andanavbar)

If you're a high-tech consumer AndoverNet should rate a permanent bookmark. If you're just curious you owe yourself at least one visit.

Technology Advances Are Mind Blowers

I came away from the opening address at SeyboldBoston, a major computer software show, a changed person. My mind was blown.

Although I only subjected myself to a two-hour opening address and a half-hour question and answer session I had more than enough to occupy my mind, fill it and then overflow it. One of the keynote speakers, Chuck Geschke of Adobe Systems, closed his remarks with the apt warning "You ain't seen nothing yet."

Surely this must be the byword of the Internet age. Everything is new. Everything immediately begins to age. The next version comes right behind. The cycle doesn't stop. Never slows down. Blink and you will have missed something important.

I didn't blink much that morning but I'm sure I missed important stuff. What I can tell you — painting with a very broad brush — is this:

What's coming is a convergence — don't you love the way these new words kangaroo their way into everyday speech? — of all communication tools in common use.

You may find it hard to conceive but the Web pages you've become used to will very rapidly begin to look more like television. There's going to be motion, action, video, sound. If you can imagine it, it'll be online within a matter of months.

According to Dan Rode, of Branestorm Internet Solutions, the average small business Web page cost $13,500 to "build" in 1997 while Fortune 500 companies spent an average of $63,000 to develop their sites. This price is going to plummet as more powerful software comes on the market.

If your business doesn't have a Web page today it will have one very soon. You're likely the one to be building it too. And no it won't be rocket science. It's going to be fun, easy and extraordinarily sophisticated by current standards. Won't cost much more than $1,000 including both time and software.

The cycle doesn't stop. Never slows down. Blink — and you've missed something important.

Much of the energy behind this extraordinary push for technical improvement comes from the realization that the Internet itself is being changed by its own growth. Branestorm estimated there were 28 million Internet users in 1996, 47 million in '97 and projected 175 million in 2002.

The future growth is almost here already.

The Irish Internet survey company, NuaNet, estimates there were already 153 million Internet users worldwide in February '99 with 87 million of them in Canada and the US.

Their results are closely mirrored by a report in early January from the Pew Research Center which showed that 41% of Americans now go online regularly and 35% use email — up from only 10% in 1995.

A more telling statistic is that two years earlier technology news was the top attraction for Web users seeking information online; now the top attraction is weather. The truth is, the average Internet user is less like the older white male academic who started it all and more like your next door neighbor — whoever she is.

Computer software and hardware developers recognize this trend. Their new products are going to be more utilitarian, easier to use, and aimed at producing something beneficial for the every-expanding market.

What each individual company was offering is not as important as the overall thrust. Change is continuing. The rate of change is accelerating. The software we have available today is amazing. What's coming is fantastic. Fasten your seatbelts and prepare for lift-off.

I told you my mind was blown but I realize that expression dates me as one of the fuddy-duddies of the past who had first hand experience with vacuum tubes before the introduction of transistors. I suppose the younger generation max out their buffers when they hit sensory overload.

I didn't even know enough to ask.

SeyboldBoston (http://www.seyboldseminars.com/)
Branestorm (http://www.branestorm.com/conference/facts.htm)
NuaNet (http://www.nua.net/surveys/how_many_online/index.html)
Pew Research Center (http://www.people-press.org/tech98sum.htm)

... two years earlier technology news was the top attraction for Web users seeking information online; now the top attraction is weather.

New Economy Spawns Voca-Web-ulary

With all the changes going on in business you'd think there would be at least some kind of cheat-sheet for managers who are feeling overwhelmed.

(And how can any manager not feel overwhelmed when you consider that the workforce now includes people old enough to have learned to calculate on a slide rule and people young enough to have never even seen one?)

Riding to the rescue of techno-peasants everywhere is Wired Magazine's Encyclopedia of the New Economy, written by editors John Browning and Spencer Reiss.

Admittedly there are those of us who feel that Wired Magazine itself sometimes needs a little riding to the rescue (I'm waiting for the text only version before I'll subscribe to the printed edition) but their ENE is a big help in deciphering the buzzwords of the new economy.

You can order a "Special Limited Edition" of the ENE from Wired Reprints online (described unabashedly as "the perfect business gift") or you can click through the 90 terms online. The definitions are extensive and sometimes complex.

In the interests of speeding along this accelerating voca-Web-ulary, we have provided samples below with our take on what they mean. (We could be wrong; we still have an abacus. Go to Wired for the official word.)

Adhocracy: "... an organization without structure ... instead of fixed tasks and job descriptions, everyone does what needs to be done." (Works better in informal settings in small groups; single parents of small children will thrive; people with insecurities, egos and ambitions will feel uncomfortable.)

Attention Economics: "... while information is essentially infinite, demand for it is limited by the waking hours in a human day." (Sleep has to be viewed as a resource that recharges eyeballs so they can absorb more advertising.)

Riding to the rescue of techno-peasants every-where is Wired Magazine's Ency-clopedia of the New Economy...

Ecash: "... encrypted electronic data redeemable for real money... cheerful, anonymous and cheap to administer..." (The more coins that pile up on your bureau the more likely you are becoming part of the Ecash economy.)

Economies of Time: "... faster is better... by learning your way of doing things, customers make a mental investment in your product ..." (General Bedford Forest said it best, the battle is won by the man who gets there "firstest with the mostest." Hence vaporware leads to betaware leads to software.)

Information Food Chain: "... data, information, knowledge." (There's a difference. You want people who have analyzed the data, digested the information, and assembled the knowledge so you can take intelligent action; now you know why we have middle managers.)

Just-in-Time Learning: "Knowledge at your fingertips ... does for knowledge what just-in-time delivery does for manufacturing..." (You can't afford to hire people who already know everything; you need to hire people who know how to find what they need to know when they need it.)

Law of One Price: "... in efficient markets, differences in price for the same item will tend toward zero." (The Internet is the great leveler and prices that can be searched and compared worldwide by computer have already begun to fall; great for consumers, tough on businesses.)

Shrinkage: "Smaller is beautiful." (Maybe hard to take if you've personally been 'downsized' but the apparent result of increasingly smaller companies is a surge in global innovation, competition and efficiency.)

Ubiquity: "Be there now." (The Internet allows you to present your information — and product — to the consumer at the moment she decides that her want has become her need: the buy moment! If you're not there you lose.)

Encyclopedia of the New Economy (http://www.hotwired.com/special/ene/index.html)

General Bedford Forest said it best, the battle is won by the man who gets there "firstest with the mostest."

WebPointers Law of Computer Problems Revealed

After years of patient research and a week of "interesting experiences" — the kind one is supposed to learn from — I am prepared to expound WebPointers Law: No one need wait for computer problems: they're on their way.

To this basic foundation of computer knowledge you may add the following three Catbird Corollaries:

1) the likelihood of a computer crash increases in direct proportion to the importance of the job being produced and in inverse proportion to the square of the time remaining for it to be accomplished

2) the probability of the data being recently saved or backed up just before the crash is directly related to the probability that pigs will fly

3) your ability to talk to a live person who can provide technical assistance erodes in direct proportion to the increasing popularity of voicemail.

My new found wisdom does not quite come like a lightning bolt out of the blue although it was a pre-dawn lightning bolt two weeks ago — in the middle of winter for God's sake! — that gave me religion.

Our underground telephone cable took a hit somewhere up the line. One of our computers, brand new out of the box less than a week earlier, didn't have its modem cable routed through a surge protector and the modem was fried.

The telephone lineman replaced their fuse. We installed a new modem. For some reason it would not connect. A day of voicemail hell and tech non-support drove us into deep despair that was only relieved when we were able to summon Cousin Armistead to come out and save us.

Armistead makes his living straightening out the tangled wires in other people's lives. His is a noble calling and he's very good at it. (Everyone needs someone like him in the family.)

He fixed our problems and made sure they wouldn't recur. Thanks to him, a Rastafarian tangle of wires cascading from the hind parts of a PC alongside a sandwich-sized Zip-drive and an all-in-one printer, copier, scanner, fax machine, are now all connected to a UPS —

...the probability of the data being recently saved or backed up just before the crash is directly related to the probability that pigs will fly.

Uninterruptible Power Supply — which in turn is plugged into our electrical outlet and telephone jack.

In the event of a complete power failure we will now have enough constant battery power to provide at least five or six minutes to save files, close programs and shut down our computers. A lightning strike should now be harmless. The unseen danger of sudden increases or decreases in voltage (spikes, sags, brownouts, blackouts, surges and noise) has also been eliminated.

Although I was aware of UPS systems years ago I didn't realize they had come down so much in price as to be in the range of Small Office Home Office entrepreneurs. Not only are they cheaper, they're more powerful and reliable. They're not just for the big guys anymore.

Better still, the companies that make them have begun to provide superb resources on the Web that not only sell the product but explain the need and reasons behind them. For instance, American Power Conversion, the Rhode Island manufacturer of our muscly little UPS, provides a major data dump on its own products but some very helpful explanations of power problems in general.

A lightning strike, such as the one we encountered, is described as traveling "instantaneously through wiring, network, serial and phone lines and more, with the electrical equivalent force of a tidal wave. The surge travels into your computer via the outlet or phone lines. The first casualty is usually a modem or motherboard. Chips go next, and data is lost." (Been there. Done that.)

APC provides a simple online form that allows you to calculate Return on Investment — the payback time for buying your UPS — and a simple quiz to determine if your risk is average, above average or high.

As the utilities struggle with increasing and shifting demands for power we all ought to be looking at increasing levels of safety for the essential equipment that controls our lives. After all, computer problems are on their way to us all, ready or not.

American Power Conversion (http://www.apcc.com)

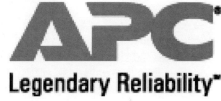

A lightning strike should now be harmless. The unseen danger of sudden increases or decreases in voltage ... has also been eliminated.

Website Appendix

401 Kafé FAQ (http://www.401kafe.com/faq/index.html)

401 Kafé: Ted's Bio (http://www.401kafe.com/tips/teds_bio.html)

401 Kafé: Ted's Table (http://www.401kafe.com/tips/teds_table.html)

401 Kafé: What's Brewing (http://www.401kafe.com/tips/brewing.html)

401 Kafé (http://www.401kafe.com/)

A Webmaster's Guide to Search Engines (http://www.searchenginewatch.com/webmasters/index.html)

Abbey of Gethsemani (http://www.monks.org/)

ABCs of 401(k) Plans (http://www.401kafe.com/education/abc_intro.html)

AltaVista (http://www.altavista.com)

AltaVista Help—Add a Page to(http://www.altavista.com/av/content/addurl.htm)

Amazon.com (http://www.amazon.com)

American Bankruptcy Institute (http://www.abiworld.org/media/newmediafront.html)

American Power Conversion (http://www.apcc.com)

AndoverNet (http://www.andover.net)

Apply to the BizRate Program (http://www.bizrate.com/MerchantOnly/merchant_terms.html)

Archetypes Storytelling Cards (http://www.thecards.com/)

Armchair Millionaire (http://www.armchairmillionaire.com)

AtYourOffice (http://www.atyouroffice.com)

Auction Tribune (http://auctiontribune.com)

Automatic Complaint Letter Generator (http://www-csag.cs.uiuc.edu/individual/pakin/complaint)

BestCalls.com (http://www.bestcalls.com)

BigCharts.com (http://www.bigcharts.com/)

Binary Compass Enterprises (http://www.binarycompass.com/)

Bizmove.com (http://www.bizmove.com/)

BizProWeb (http://www.bizproweb.com)

BizProWeb Features library (http://www.bizproweb.com/pages/features/features.html)

BizProWeb Forums (http://www.bizproweb.com/pages/forums/index.shtml)

BizProWeb Shareware (http://www.bizproweb.com/pages/shareware/shareware.html)

BizRate (http://www.bizrate.com)

Blue Mountain Arts (http://www.bluemountain.com/index.html)

Brain Boot Camp (http://www.botree.com/boot/index.htm)

Branestorm (http://www.branestorm.com/conference/facts.htm)

Bureau of Labor Statistics (http://stats.bls.gov/blshome.html)

Business and Professional Newsgroups (http://www.bizproweb.com/pages/newsgroups/newsgroups_home.html)

Business and Professional Websites (http://www.bizproweb.com/pages/websites/websites_home.html)

Business Hotlinks (http://www.score.org/businesslinks)

Business Resources Index (http://www.score.org/resourceindex/resource.html)

BuyersZone (http://www.buyerszone.com)

C-call.com (http://www.c-call.com/)

CardWeb (http://www.cardweb.com)

CareerPath (http://www.careerpath.com)

Case Studies: False Statements (http://rider.wharton.upenn.edu/~ethics/cases/false.htm)

Chronological List (http://www.thestreet.com/basics/countdown/748433.html)

Client Sucessses (http://www.score.org/success)

Cluetrain buzz (http://www.cluetrain.com/buzz.html)

Cluetrain Manifesto (http://www.cluetrain.com/)

Cluetrain Ringleaders (http://www.cluetrain.com/ringleaders.html)

Companies of the Dow (http://www.bd.dowjones.com/category.asp?CatID=2)

Competitive Intelligence Guide (http://www.fuld.com)

Computers.com (http://www.computers.com)

Consumer Credit Counseling Service (http://www.powersource.com/cccs/default.html)

Consumer Price Index Inflation Calculator (http://www.jsc.nasa.gov/bu2/inflateCPI.html)

Cool Tool of the Day (http://www.CoolTool.com/index.html?at000en_andanavbar)

Corporate America's Most Powerful People (http://www.forbes.com/tool/toolbox/ceo/)

Craig Sonnenberg (http://www.bizproweb.com/pages/about/about.html)

Current Value of Old Money (http://www.exeter.ac.uk/~RDavies/aria/current/howmuhc.html)

Cyberculture (http://www.whatis.com/cybercul.htm)

Daily Wealth Index (http://www.forbes.com/gates/daily.asp)

Dave Central (http://www.HardwareWatch.com/index.html?ann000en_andanavbar)

DealDeal (http://dealdeal.com/)

Deepavali Cards (http://www.tamilpages.com/greetingcards/diwali.shtml)

Deja News (http://www.dejanews.com)

Device for Helping Late Commuters (http://www.rube-goldberg.com/card4.gif)

Dharma the Cat (http://www.dharmathecat.com/)

Diwali (http://india.indiagov.org/culture/festival/diwali.htm)

Dow Jones Business Directory (http://www.bd.dowjones.com)

Drugstore.com (http://www.drugstore.com)

E-stamp.com (http://www.e-stamp.com)

eBay (http://www.ebay.com)

EgoSurf (http://www.egosurf.com)

Encyclopedia of the New Economy (http://www.hotwired.com/special/ene/index.html)

Enigma (http://www.twintrees.demon.co.uk/minfo.html)

Entrepreneur's Mind Archives(http://www.benlore.com/files/archive.html)

Entrepreneur Test (http://www.bizmove.com/other/quiz/htm)

Entrepreneur's Mind (http://www.benlore.com/index2.html)

Envelope Manager (http://www.envmgr.com)

Excite (http://www.excite.com)

Executive PayWatch (http://aflcio.org/paywatch/)

Executive PayWatch Database (http://aflcio.org/cgi-bin/aflcio.pl)

Experts Corner (http://www.benlore.com/files/emexpert2_1.html)

Explore the Internet (http://lcweb.loc.gov/global/explore.html)

Fish an Olive Out of a Long-Necked Bottle (http://www.rube-goldberg.com/card3.gif)

Five Steps to Financial Freedom (http://www.armchairmillionaire.com/fivesteps/)

Flying Noodle (http://www.flyingnoodle.com)

Forbes 400 (http://www.forbes.com/forbes/Section/400.htm)

Forbes Magazine (http://www.forbes.com)

Ford Motor Company (http://www2.ford.com)

Forum Discussion in Fast Company (http://www.fastcompany.com/online/14/intelligence.html)

Franklin-Templeton (http://www.franklin-templeton.com/)

Free Code (http://www.FreeCode.com/index.html?at000en_andanavbar)

Fuld's Corporate Evaluation Questionnaire (http://www.fuld.com/StrategiesCorpEval.html)

Fuld's Intelligence Dictionary (http://www.fuld.com/Dictionary/index.html)

Fuld's Internet Intelligence Index (http://www.fuld.com/i3/index.html)

Gallery of Investors (http://www.armchairmillionaire.com/gallery/)

Get Email Counseling (http://www.score.org/online/)

Global Financial Data (http://www.globalfindata.com/tbukcpi.htm)

Global Perspective (http://www.benlore.com/files/emglobal2_1.html)

Government Publications (http://lcweb.loc.gov/rr/news/lcgovd.html)

Great Books (http://www.amazon.com/exec/obidos/ISBN=0684835339/4805-9632618-739203)

Grocery Shopping Network (http://grocerywebsites.com/)

Growing a Business on the Internet (http://www.bizmove.com/internet/main.htm)

Habitat for Humanity (http://www.habitat.org/)

Hallmark (http://www.hallmarkconnections.com/)

HardwareWatch (http://www.HardwareWatch.com/index.html?an000en_andanavbar)

HomeGrocer.com (http://www.homegrocer.com)

Homeruns (http://www.homeruns.com/)

Hot Rod Your Head (http://www.botree.com/)

HotBot (http://www.hotbot.com)

How to suggest a site to Yahoo! (http://www.yahoo.com/info/suggest/)

HyperData (http://www.hyperdatadirect.com/)

Iconocast Internet Marketing Newsletter (http://www.iconocast.com/)

Imprint Magazine's Online Editorial (http://www.logomall.com/imprintPM/issues/current/editorial.htm)

Inflation Calculator (http://www.westegg.com/inflation)

InGenius Technologies (http://www.ingetech.com)

Inspirational Stuff (http://www.bizmove.com/inspiring.htm)

Inst. for the Study of Applied and Professional Ethics (http://www.dartmouth.edu/artsci/ethicsinst/)

Internet Movie Database (http://www.imdb.com)

Internet Traffic Report (http://www.andovernews.com/trafficreport.html?at000en_andanavbar)

IPrint (http://www.iprint.com)

IQ Tests (http://www.botree.com/iq.htm)

JavElink (http://www.javelink.com)

Jerry's Foods (http://www.jerrysfoods.com/faxmail.htm)

John Templeton Foundation (http://www.templeton.org/)

Just for Fun (http://www.studeo.com/flash/index.html)

KeyBank (http://www.key.com/)

Keynote Entrepreneur (http://www.benlore.com/fiels/emkey2_1.html)

L.L. Bean (http://www.llbean.com/)

L.L. Bean Corporate Sales (http://www.llbean.com/corporateSales/index.noframes.html)

Lands' End (http://www.landsend.com)

Lands' End Corporate Sales (http://www.landsend.com/corpsales/)

Launch Pad (http://www.benlore.com/files/emlaunch2_1.html)

Library of Congress (http://loc.gov/)

Library of Congress Research and Reference (http://loc.gov/rr/research.html)

LiveBid (http://www.livebid.com)

Logomall's Promotional Products Reference Guide (http://www.logomall.com/about/APP1.HTM)

Magellan (http://www.mckinley.com/)

Magellan Search Voyeur (http://voyeur.mckinley.com/cgi-bin/voyeur.cgi)

MailStart (http://www.mailstart.com)

Managing a Small Business (http://www.bizmove.com/other/cdpage.htm)

MediaBuilder (http://www.MediaBuilder.com/index.html)

Model Portfolio (http://www.armchairmillionaire.com/portfolio/)

Money Management International (http://www.mmintl.org/)

MoneyWise (http://www.mmintl.org/news/default.html)

Monster Board (http://www.monsterboard.com)

MVRD Investment and Online Banking Resources (http://www.refdesk.com/online.html)

MySimon (http://www.mySimon.com)

Needle's Eye Ministries (http://www.zip2.com/styleweekly/needleseye)

Neopost (http://www.neopost.com)

NetBrief (http://www.netbrief.com)

NetGrocer (http://www.netgrocer.com/)

New Technology (http://www.whatis.com/newtech.htm)

News of The Weird Archives (http://www.nine.org/notw/archives.html)

Newspaper & Periodical Reading Room (http://lcweb.loc.gov/rr/news)

NextCard (http://www.nextcard.com)

No More Oversleeping (http://www.rube-goldberg.com/card1.gif)

NuaNet (http://www.nua.net/surveys/how_many_online/index.html)

Numerical List (http://www.thestreet.com/basics/countdown/747965.html)

Occupations with Largest Job Growth(http://stats.bls.gov/news.release/ecopro.table7.htm)

Office Depot (http://www.officedepot.com)

Office.com (http://www.office.com)

OfficeMax (http://www.officemax.com)

Official Federal Government Web Sites (http://lcweb.loc.gov/global/executive/fed.html)

Official Rube Goldberg Website (http://www.rube-goldberg.com/rg2idx.htm)

Olleyowl (http://www.angelfire.com/ak/olly/greeting.html)

Online News Page Archives (http://www.journalist.org/cgi-bin/online-news/online_news/index.html)

Onlineofficesupplies (http://www.onlineofficesupplies.com)

Onsale (http://www.onsale.com/)

Oregon Cupboard (http://www.oregoncupboard.com/)

PeachTree Network (http://www.thepeachtree.net)

Peapod (http://www.peapod.com/)

Pets.com (http://www.pets.com)

Pew Research Center (http://www.people-press.org/tech98sum.htm)

Picks of the Day (http://www.bizproweb.com/pages/picks/picks_of_the_day.html)

Pitney Bowes (http://www.pb.com)

PlanetAll (http://www.planetall.com)

Poor Rich's Almanac (http://www.armchairmillionaire.com/poorrich/)

PromoCity (http://www.promocity.com/premiums.htm)

Promotional Media (http://www.promotionalmedia.com/hotel.html)

Queenan Article (http://www.forbes.com/forbes/97/1013/6008046a.htm)

Rube Goldberg Machine Contest (http://www.purdue.edu/UNS/rube/rube.index.html)

Runaway CEO Pay (http://aflcio.org/paywatch/ceopay.htm)

SCORE (http://www.score.org)

Search Engine Watch (http://www.searchenginewatch.com/)

SeyboldBoston (http://www.seyboldseminars.com/)

Shoplink (http://www.shoplink.com/)

Signature-mail (http://www.signature-mail.com/)

Slaughterhouse (http://www.SlaughterHouse.com/index.html?at000en_andanavbar)

Small Business Directory (http://www.bizmove.com/directory/index.htm)

Small Business Knowledge Base (http://www.bizmove.com)

Society of Competitive Intelligence Professionals (http://www.scip.org)

Solemates (http://www.centuryinshoes.com/)

Stamps.com (http://www.stamps.com)

Staples (http://www. staples.com)

Student Advantage (http://www.studentadvantage.com/)

Studeo.com (http://www.studeo.com/)

Survey of Executive Compensation (http://www.forbes.com/forbes/99/0517/6310202a.htm)

Tech Web (http://www.techweb.com/)

Templeton Prize (http://templeton.org/prize/default.asp)

The Abbey of New Clairvaux (http://www.maxinet.com/trappist/)

The Basics of Business History (http://www.thestreet.com/basics/countdown/747895.html)

The Competitive Edge (http://www.compet.com/coffeemugs.html)

The Economist (http://www.economist.com)

TheStreet.com (http://www.thestreet.com)

TheStreet.com Reader Feedback (http://www.thestreet.com/basics/countdown/747986.html)

This Is True (http://www.thisistrue.com)

Tulip Bulb Speculation (http://www.derivatives.com/comix/1996/9602/9602cx1.html)

Turbonium (http://www.turbonium.com/flash/index.html)

Twin Peaks Gourmet Trading Post (http://tpeaks.com/)

Typospace (http://www.yugop.com/typospace.html#)

University of Texas Winning Device (http://www.purdue.edu/UNS/html4ever/970405.Rube.natl.html)

University of British Columbia's Centre for Applied Ethics (http://www.ethics.ubc.ca/)

University of Virginia's Olsson Center (http://www.darden.virginia.edu/research/olsson/olsson.htm)

Using the Internet (http://www.whatis.com/using.htm)

Vcall (http://www.vcall.com)

Wachovia PC Access (http://www.wachovia.com/pcaccess/index.html)

Wacky Uses (http://www.wackyuses.com)

Web Lab (http://www.weblab.org)

WebCrawler (http://webcrawler.com/)

WebCrawler Help: Add URL (http://www.WebCrawler.com/Help/GetListed/AddURLS.html)

WebCrawler Search Voyeur (http://webcrawler.com/SearchTicker.html)

Wharton Business School Zicklin Center (http://rider.wharton.upenn.edu/~ethics/zicklin/research.html)

Wharton's Newsletter (http://rider.wharton.upenn.edu/~ethics/newsletter/fall97news1.pdf)

Whatis.com (http://www.whatis.com)

WinStar Communications, Inc. (http://www.winstar.com)

Working Mom's Internet Refuge (http://www.moms-refuge.com)

Working Stiff (http://www.pbs.org/weblab/workingstiff/)

Yahoo! (http://www.yahoo.com)

Yahoo! How-To Resources, Web Design, etc. (http://howto.yahoo.com/resources/html_guides)

Yomega Corp (http://www.yomega.com/)

Index

The design for WebPointers Essential Business Websites reflects the influence of Master Typographer Jan Tschichold. The horizontal proportions were chosen to offer the best onscreen presentation for the companion eBook Edition which is published in Adobe Software's Portable Document Format. Text is typeset in Gill Sans, headlines in Giovanni Book. Printing and binding by Lithocolor Press Inc. of Westchester, Illinois.

About the Authors

Kitty Williams and Robin Lind are lifelong journalists whose syndicated newspaper column, WebPointers, has been published in a growing number of newspapers since February, 1996.

Educated in America and Europe, they are both graduates of the University of Virginia. They live in central Virginia's James River Valley.

The first in the Essential Websites series, "WebPointers Essential NetNovice Websites," ISBN 0-9639531-5-X, was published by Hope Springs Press in February, 1999.

For more information visit WebPointers Online
http://www.webpointers.com